# 跨境电商入门一本通
## （汉英对照）

陈一宁 编著

Cross-Border
E-Commerce
All-in-One (Bilingual)

浙江工商大学出版社
ZHEJIANG GONGSHANG UNIVERSITY PRESS
·杭州·

# 前　言

．．．．．．．．．．．．．．．．．．．．．．．．．．．．．．．．．．．．．．．．．．．．．．．．．．．．．．．．．．．．．．．．．．．．．．．．．．．．．．
．．．．．．．．．．．．．．．．．．．．．．．．．．．．．．．．．．．．．．．．．．．．．．．．．．．．．．．．．．．．．．．．．．．．．．．．．．．．．．

近年来，随着互联网基础设施的完善和全球性物流网络的构建，跨境电商交易规模一直保持着高增长率。跨境电商行业的迅猛发展促使企业需要大量既懂外语又懂外贸业务的专业人才。我国政府、各大高校和协会也在多方助力跨境电商人才的培养，以满足当地跨境电商企业的人才需求，推动数字经济的发展。鉴于越来越多的中外读者开始关注跨境电商英语方面的知识，但市场上鲜有跨境电商双语读本，笔者结合多年的教学经验，撰写了这本双语读本，以便教学与研究。

本读本以中英文双语对照为特色，旨在满足零基础、想了解或从事跨境电商业务新手的需求，以及想在跨境电商行业创业或就业的来自"一带一路"沿线国家或其他英语国家留学生的需求。除此之外，该读本还适合跨境电商双语专业的师生、援外跨境电商项目培训机构以及中小外贸企业拓展跨境电商业务员工等使用。

本读本集跨境电商基础和实战为一体，语言通俗易懂，话题覆盖面广，案例丰富实用，章节划分合理，为初学者入门起到了很好的引导作用。第一章是跨境电商概述，分别概述了跨境电商的含义、特点、意义和专业人才素质；第二章是跨境电商运营平台，包括速卖

## Cross-Border
# E-Commerce
## All-in-One (Bilingual)

通、亚马逊、Wish 和易贝四个平台的特点、店铺注册和产品管理等内容;第三章是跨境电商营销,含有跨境市场分析及各跨境电商营销模式,帮助跨境电商卖家更好地了解和选择营销模式,增加销量;第四章是跨境电商物流,介绍了不同的物流模式和物流选择,帮助跨境电商卖家化解物流难题;第五章是跨境电商客服,帮助跨境电商卖家提升客户服务质量,增加客户黏性;附录介绍的是其他跨境电商平台的基本信息。

在编写过程中,编者参阅了相关专著和教材,相关参考内容已列入参考文献,在此向诸位表示衷心的感谢。此外,由于编者水平有限、时间不足,作为跨境电子商务领域探索性双语读本,定不乏偏颇、疏漏及不足之处,希望业内专家、读者不吝指正。

本读本作为研究基金项目,得到了浙江省社科联社科普及项目(课题编号20KPD31YB)的资助,特此感谢!

编 者

2019 年 9 月

# Content

# Chapter One
## Overview of Cross-Border E-Commerce

跨境电商概述

## Lead-in

## 导入

In 2018, the total scale of import and export by way of cross-border e-commerce reached RMB 9.1 trillion, a year-on-year increase of 11.6%, with over 100 million users in total. From the perspective of trading mode, Chinese B2B cross-border e-commerce transactions accounted for 83.2%, and B2C cross-border e-commerce transactions accounted for 16.8%. From the perspective of import and export structure, China's cross-border e-commerce exports accounted for 78.9% of the total, and the import ratio was 21.1%. The market is still dominated by exports. This chapter will introduce the concept, development and characteristics, significance and talent qualities of cross-border e-commerce.

2018年,中国跨境电商交易规模达9.1万亿元,同比增长11.6%,用户规模超1亿。从交易模式来看,我国跨境电商B2B交易占比达83.2%,跨境电商B2C交易占比达16.8%。从进出口结构来看,我国跨境电商的出口占比达78.9%,进口比例为21.1%,出口依然占据主导地位。本章会依次介绍跨境电商的含义、发展和特点、意义以及专业人才素质等知识。

## Section One / **Concept of Cross-Border E-Commerce**

## 跨境电商的含义

Cross-border e-commerce, refers to an international business activity that the transaction entities in different customs area and electronizes the traditional trade in terms of products display, negotiation and transaction through the means of e-commerce, making payment and settlement through e-commerce platforms, as well as delivering products through cross-border logistics or international warehousing services to complete the transaction. In fact, cross-border e-commerce is an emerging international trade model that innovates the traditional one. It uses the electronic trading platform as the basis and electronic payment and logistics as the means to transfer traditional sales and shopping channels to the Internet, breaking the barrier between the states and the regions, which aims to earn foreign exchanges.

跨境电商指分属于不同关境的交易主体,通过电子商务手段将传统进出口贸易中的展示、洽谈和成交环节电子化,进行支付结算,并通过跨境物流或异地仓储送达商品、完成交易的一种国际商业活动。实际上,跨境电商是一种新兴的国际贸易模式,是对传统国际贸易模式的创新,将电子交易平台作为基础,以电子支付和物流为手段,把传统的销售、购物渠道转移到互联网上,打破国家与地区间的壁垒,用以赚取外汇的一种贸易方式。

As shown in Figure 1-1, the basic process of cross-border e-commerce includes four main entities, that is, authorities, intermediary agencies, customers and suppliers. Customers purchase goods through cross-border e-commerce platforms and pay suppliers who deliver the goods accordingly. Authorities play the role of supervision and policy guidance, and intermediary agencies mainly provide third-party platforms or comprehensive services.

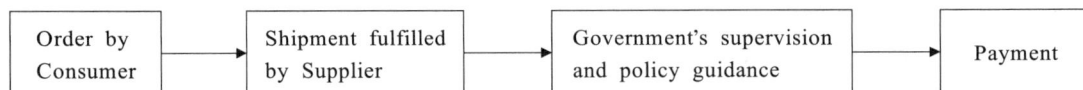

| Order by Consumer | → | Shipment fulfilled by Supplier | → | Government's supervision and policy guidance | → | Payment |
| --- | --- | --- | --- | --- | --- | --- |

Figure 1-1　Procedure of Cross-Border E-Commerce

如图1-1所示,跨境电商的基本流程包括四个主体——政府部门、中间机构、顾客和供应商。顾客通过跨境电商平台购买商品,并支付货款给供应商,供应商发货,政府部门进行监管和政策引导,中间机构主要提供第三方平台或综合服务。

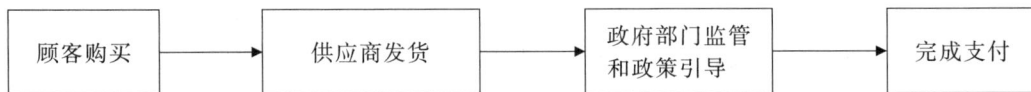

| 顾客购买 | → | 供应商发货 | → | 政府部门监管和政策引导 | → | 完成支付 |
| --- | --- | --- | --- | --- | --- | --- |

图1-1　跨境电商流程图

In terms of transaction entities, cross-border e-commerce can be divided into B2B cross-border e-commerce, B2C cross-border e-commerce, and C2C cross-border e-commerce. In terms of commodity category of platforms and e-commerce websites' development and operation subjects, cross-border e-commerce can be divided into four types: integrated platform, comprehensive direct sales, vertical platform and vertical direct sales. In terms of customs area, it can be divided into import cross-border e-commerce and export cross-border e-commerce.

从交易主体的角度划分,可以将跨境电商分为B2B跨境电商、B2C跨境电商和C2C跨境电商三类。从平台经营商品品类和电子商务网站开发与运营主体的角度划分,可以将跨境电商分为综合平台型、综合自营型、垂直平台型和垂直自营型四类。从关境角度分类,可划分为跨境进口电商和跨境出口电商两类。

## 1. B2B Cross-Border E-Commerce（B2B跨境电商）

B2B (Business-to-Business) cross-border e-commerce is an international business activity between companies in different customs areas. The process includes reaching the transaction, completing the payment and settlement through e-commerce platform, delivering goods through cross-border logistics, and completing transactions. B2B cross-border e-commerce includes not only the online trading part through cross-border trading platform, but also the part that realizes offline trading through online trading. The most representative platform is Alibaba (1688 Global Shopping Website).

B2B跨境电商,是指分属不同关境的企业通过电商平台达成交易,进行支付结算,并通过跨境物流送达商品、完成交易的一种国际商业活动。B2B跨境电商不仅包括通过跨境交易平台实现的线上交易部分,还包括通过线上交易撮合实现线下交易的部分,最具有代表性的是阿里巴巴(1688全球购物网站)。

## 2. B2C Cross-Border E-Commerce（B2C跨境电商）

B2C (Business-to-Consumer) cross-border e-commerce refers to the international business activity of companies in different customs areas, directly selling products or services to consumers through e-commerce platform. The process includes reaching the transactions, completing payment and settlement, delivering products through cross-border logistics, and completing the transaction. The most representative ones are Tmall Global, NetEase Koala, and JD Global, etc.

跨境零售中的B2C跨境电商是指分属不同关境的企业直接面向消费者个人开展在线销售产品和服务,通过电商平台达成交易、进行支付结算,并通过跨境物流送达商品、完成交易的一种国际商业活动。B2C跨境电商中具有代表性的有天猫国际、网易考拉、京东全球购等。

## 3. C2C Cross-Border E-Commerce（C2C跨境电商）

C2C (Consumer-to-Consumer) cross-border e-commerce refers to the international business activity between individual buyers and individual sellers in different customs territory. Individual sellers publish the products, prices, etc., through third-party e-commerce platforms, and the individual buyers select the products. The process includes reaching the transactions, completing payment settlement, and delivering products through cross-border logistics, and completing the transactions. AliExpress, eBay and Wish are representatives of C2C cross-border e-commerce.

C2C 跨境电商是指分属不同关境的个人卖方对个人买方开展在线销售产品和服务，由个人卖家通过第三方电商平台发布售卖产品信息、价格等内容，个人买方进行筛选，最终通过电商平台达成交易、进行支付结算，并通过跨境物流送达商品、完成交易的一种国际商业活动。C2C 跨境电商中具有代表性的有速卖通、易贝、Wish 等。

## 4. Vertical & Integrated Cross-Border E-Commerce（垂直型跨境电商与综合型跨境电商）

Vertical cross-border e-commerce refers to an e-commerce model that deepens operations in a certain industry or market segment. Vertical e-commerce sites focus on B2C or B2B businesses of similar products in certain areas, such as Vipshop, which focuses on women's products.

垂直型跨境电商是指在某一个行业或细分市场深化运营的电子商务模式。垂直电子商务网站专注于某些特定领域同类产品的 B2C 或者 B2B 业务，如专注女性用品特卖的唯品会。

Integrated cross-border e-commerce, also known as horizontal cross-border e-commerce, provides online operations for multi-industry products, which is comprehensive and similar to online shopping malls. It is designed to provide users with wide product line and comparable commercial services, such as Tmall Global, JD Global and so on.

综合型跨境电商，又称水平型跨境电商，提供多行业产品的网上经营，综合性强，类似于网上购物中心，旨在为用户提供产品线宽、可比性强的商业服务，如天猫国际、京东全球购等。

## 5. Platform & Direct Sales Cross-Border E-Commerce（平台型电商与自营型电商）

Platform cross-border e-commerce refers to the development and operation of e-commerce platforms on the Internet, which attracts merchants and charges them a certain fee as the profit model, but platforms do not engage in commodities procurement, sales, etc., such as Wish.

平台型跨境电商是指在线上开发和运营电子商务平台，吸引商家入驻，以收取商家一定费用作为盈利模式，但并不从事商品采购、销售等工作，如 Wish 等。

Direct sales cross-border e-commerce refers to the development and operation of an e-commerce platform on the Internet, covering the entire supply chain from merchandise procurement, stocking, supply, sales to after-sales, such as Amazon Overseas, etc.

自营型跨境电商是指在线上开发和运营电子商务平台，涉及从商品采购、备货、供应、销售到售后的整条供应链，如亚马逊海外购等。

## Section Two / Development and Characteristics of Cross-Border E-Commerce in China
## 中国跨境电商发展和特点

### 1. Development of Cross-Border E-Commerce in China（中国跨境电商发展）

In 1995, e-commerce was created. In 1999, Alibaba was established. After connecting Chinese suppliers and overseas buyers via the Internet, Internet-based international trading methods first appeared. With the continuous development of global information technology, cross-border e-commerce is rapidly developing as a hot emerging trading method.

1995年，电子商务诞生。1999年，阿里巴巴成立。通过互联网连接中国供应商与海外买家后，互联网化的国际贸易方式首次出现。随着全球信息技术的不断发展，跨境电商作为一种热门的新兴贸易方式，正在迅速崛起。

Up to now, China's cross-border e-commerce has experienced three stages of development. After the 1.0 stage information service era and the 2.0 stage online transaction era, it is now entering the 3.0 stage characterized by full-industry chain services.

截至目前，我国跨境电商共经历了三个发展阶段，从1.0阶段的信息服务时代进入到2.0阶段的在线交易时代之后，目前正在进入以全产业链服务为特征的3.0阶段。

The First Stage: Cross-Border E-Commerce 1.0 Stage (1999–2003)

From 1999 to 2003, it was the initial stage of cross-border e-commerce development in China. Its main business model is the online information service model for online display and offline transactions. In this stage, the cross-border e-commerce platform mainly provided the online display service for enterprises and products, which was equivalent to the Yellow Pages on the Internet, and still couldn't realize online transactions.

第一阶段:跨境电商 1.0 阶段(1999—2003 年)

1999—2003 年,是我国跨境电商发展起步阶段,其主要商业模式是网上展示、线下交易的外贸信息服务模式。在这个发展阶段,跨境电子商务平台主要是为企业以及产品提供网络展示平台,相当于互联网上的黄页,仍无法实现在线交易。

The platform mainly relied on membership fees from companies that displayed information to make profits. At the same time, the platform also provided suppliers with bid promotion, consulting and other services. Alibaba International Station and Global Sources Network were the typical representative platforms for this stage. Although cross-border e-commerce 1.0 stage solved the problem of how Chinese enterprises showed products to the world through the Internet, the online transaction link could not be completed due to technical restrictions, and only the information flow was integrated.

平台主要依靠向展示信息的企业收取会员费来盈利。同时,平台也为供应商提供竞价推广、咨询等服务。阿里巴巴国际站和环球资源网为此阶段的典型代表平台。跨境电商 1.0 阶段虽然通过互联网解决了中国企业向世界买家展示产品的难题,但是因技术限制无法完成在线交易环节,仅完成了信息流的整合。

The Second Stage: Cross-Border E-Commerce 2.0 Stage (2004–2012)

From 2004 to 2012, the concept of cross-border e-commerce gradually became popular, and it began to evolve from pure display to electronic process of offline transactions, payments, logistics, etc., and gradually realized online trading functions. At this stage, through direct docking of SMEs (Small and Medium Enterprises) sellers, the industry chain was further shortened, and the profit margin of commodities was increased. A large number of sellers poured into cross-border e-commerce.

第二阶段:跨境电商 2.0 阶段(2004—2012 年)

2004—2012 年,跨境电商概念逐步盛行,开始从纯展示行为发展为线下交易、支付、物流等流程电子化,逐步实现在线交易功能。这一阶段通过直接对接中小企业卖家,进一步缩短产业链,提升了商品的利润空间,大量卖家涌入跨境电商。

However, with the emergence of fake and counterfeit goods in cross-border e-commerce, international boycotts and blockades became more stringent. The third-party platform realized diversification of revenues, and charged a certain percentage of commission according to the transaction amount instead of membership fees. At the same time, it also gained value-added benefits through marketing, payment services, and logistics services on the platform. The representative platforms that developed rapidly at this stage were DHgate, LightInTheBox and so on. At this stage, the Chinese government also began to pay attention to cross-border e-commerce, intensively enact regulations, and to strengthen support.

但随着跨境电商中仿品和假货问题的出现,国际上对其的抵制和封杀也越来越严厉。第三方平台实现了营收的多元化,将收取会员费改成交易佣金模式,即按成交额来收取一定比例的佣金。同时,第三方平台还通过平台上的营销推广、支付服务、物流服务等获得增值收益。在此阶段发展迅速的平台代表有敦煌网、兰亭集势等。在此阶段,我国政府也开始重视跨境电商领域,密集颁布法规,并且加强扶持力度。

The Third Stage: Cross-Border E-Commerce 3.0 Stage (2013–Present)

2013 was an important transition year for cross-border e-commerce. Cross-border e-commerce exports have gradually formed a group of leading companies such as Alibaba, Amazon, LightInTheBox, etc., and cross-border e-commerce imports have begun to rise. The cross-border e-commerce industry chain has seen changes in terms of business models. The main models have changed from C2C and B2C to B2B and M2B. The user groups have changed from grassroots entrepreneurs to factories and foreign trade companies with strong production designs and management capabilities.

第三阶段:跨境电商3.0阶段(2013年至今)

2013年是跨境电商的重要转型年,跨境电商出口逐步形成以阿里巴巴、亚马逊、兰亭集势等为行业龙头的格局,跨境电商进口开始崛起。跨境电商全产业链都出现了商业模式的变化,主要平台模式由C2C、B2C向B2B、M2B转变,用户群体由草根创业者向具有极强的生产设计和管理能力的工厂、外贸公司转变。

A large number of traditional industrial and trade enterprises have made a difficult transition to cross-border e-commerce business. The production mode has changed from a large production line to flexible manufacturing, and the demand for operational and industrial chain supporting services is relatively high. As cross-border e-commerce gradually enters the stage of full competition, national supervision policies are increasingly perfect, and enterprises have to invest more energy in market, talent and brand building. The competition between companies changes from price to products, and now brands. In order to go global, e-commerce enterprises will build their brands based on their own advantages.

大量传统工贸企业向跨境电商业务艰难转型,生产模式由大规模生产线向灵活制造转变,对运营和产业链配套服务需求较高。随着跨境电商逐步进入充分竞争阶段,各国跨境电商监管政策日益完善,企业不得不在市场、人才和品牌建设方面投入更多精力,从比价格向比产品、比品牌转变,电商企业将依托自己的优势建立品牌,从而走向世界。

The integrated service sector of cross-border e-commerce in China has begun to take shape. The entire industry's ecosystem has become increasingly sound, and the division of labor has become increasingly clear. A number of outstanding companies like OneTouch, PingPong, Ueasychina, etc., have come to the market, mainly providing a series of professional services for cross-border e-commerce companies in terms of finance, payment, and logistics supply chain to better help cross-border e-commerce sellers and promote the rapid development of cross-border e-commerce.

我国跨境电商综合服务领域初具规模,整个行业生态体系越来越健全,分工也越来越清晰,诞生了一批像一达通、PingPong、融易通等优秀公司,主要为跨境电商企业提供金融、支付、物流供应链等一系列专业服务,从而更好地帮助跨境电商卖家,推动跨境电商快速发展。

## 2. Characteristics of Cross-Border E-Commerce in China(中国跨境电商发展的特点)

At present, China's cross-border e-commerce industry is developing rapidly, mainly reflecting the following characteristics: Firstly, the scale of cross-border e-commerce transactions continues to expand. Secondly, cross-border e-commerce is dominated by B2B services, and the B2C model is gradually emerging. Thirdly, many SMEs are engaged in cross-border trade, and the branding process is accelerating.

当前,我国跨境电子商务行业发展迅速,主要体现出以下特征:一是跨境电商交易规模持续扩大;二是跨境电商以B2B业务为主,B2C模式逐渐兴起;三是越来越多中小企业从事跨境贸易,品牌化进程加速。

(1) The Scale of Cross-Border E-Commerce Transactions Continues to Expand (跨境电商交易规模持续扩大)

As the current world trade tends to converge, more and more enterprises and merchants are beginning to reduce circulation and its costs, shorten the distance with foreign consumers to open up foreign markets, and improve economic efficiency.

Cross-border e-commerce provides a favorable channel. In recent years, as the new foreign trade model, the scale of cross-border e-commerce transactions has continued to expand.

由于当前世界贸易趋于收敛,越来越多的企业和商家开始致力于减少流通环节,降低流通成本,缩短和国外消费者的距离,以开拓国外市场,提高经济效益,而跨境电商正好为其提供了有利的渠道。近年来跨境电商作为外贸新业态,交易规模不断扩大。

In 2018, the total scale of China's import and export transactions was RMB9.1 trillion, a year-on-year increase of 11.6%. The number of users exceeded 100 million. The proportion of cross-border e-commerce accounting for import and export trade was 30%. There are more than 5,000 cross-border e-commerce platform enterprises, and more than 200,000 cross-border e-commerce companies have been launched through various platforms.

2018年中国进出口交易总规模为9.1万亿元,同比增长11.6%,用户规模超1亿,跨境电商占进出口贸易额比例为30%。跨境电商平台企业超过5000家,境内通过各类平台开展跨境电商的企业超过20万家。

(2) Cross-Border E-Commerce Is Dominated by B2B Business, and the B2C Model Is Gradually Emerging (跨境电商以B2B业务为主,B2C模式逐渐兴起)

According to the operating model, cross-border e-commerce can be divided into general trade (B2B cross-border) and cross-border online retail (B2C and C2C cross-border). As cross-border trade entities become smaller in scale and the channels between factories and consumers are diversified, cross-border transaction orders tend to be fragmented, and the proportion of B2C transactions is expected to increase in the future.

按照运营模式划分,跨境电商可分为一般贸易(B2B跨境)和跨境网络零售(B2C和C2C跨境)。随着跨境贸易主体越来越小,以及产品从工厂到消费者的途径越来越多样化,跨境交易订单趋向于碎片化和小额化,未来B2C交易占比有望进一步提升。

From the perspective of China's cross-border e-commerce transaction model in 2016, B2B cross-border transactions accounted for 86.5% of the total, occupying an absolute dominant position; in 2017, B2B cross-border e-commerce transactions accounted for 85.2%; in 2018, B2B cross-border e-commerce transactions accounted for 83.2%. The proportion dropped slightly, but overall, B2B business transactions are still in an absolute advantage in China's import and export cross-border e-commerce. In the foreseeable future, B2B is still the most important mode for Chinese enterprises to explore overseas markets.

从2016年中国跨境电商的交易模式来看,跨境B2B的交易占比为86.5%,占据绝对主导地位;2017年中国B2B跨境电商的交易占比为85.2%;2018年中国B2B跨境电商的交易占比为83.2%,比例有小幅度下降,但是从整体来看,在我国进出口跨境电商中,B2B商业交易仍然处于绝对优势的地位。可以预见,未来B2B仍然是中国企业开拓海外市场的最重要模式。

(3) More and More SMEs Are Engaged in Cross-Border Trade, and the Branding Process Is Accelerating (越来越多中小企业从事跨境贸易,品牌化进程加速)

It is estimated that among the newly registered business entities on cross-border e-commerce platform each year, SMEs and individual merchants account for over 90%. Through cross-border e-commerce, SMEs and individual merchants can reduce the intermediate links of trade and transaction costs for enterprises, make information flow freely, and expand the international market.

据估算,目前每年在跨境电商平台上新注册的经营主体中,中小企业和个体商户占到90%以上。通过跨境电商,中小企业和个体商户可以缩减贸易中间环节,降低企业交易成本,让信息更加畅通,并且拓展国际市场。

Since brand can help consumers identify, distinguish the product and service quality from other competitors, and promote consumers to continuously purchase and recommend. A large number of SMEs begin to transform products from "Made in China" to "High quality in China". By improving Quality in products, service, and independent design, we will create high value-added oversea brands, get rid of homogenization competition, realize differentiated breakout, and develop from lower end of value chain to higher end, and achieve the goal of going global.

由于品牌有利于消费者识别,区别于其他竞争者提供的产品品质和服务价值,促进客户持续购买与口碑传播的价值认同,大量中小企业也正在从"中国制造"向"中国质造"转型升级。通过提升产品品质、服务质量、独立设计,这些企业打造高附加值的出海品牌,摆脱同质化竞争,实现差异化突围,从价值链低端向上发展,实现货通全球的目标。

# Section Three / The Significance of Cross-Border E-Commerce
## 跨境电商的意义

Since 2015, the growth rate of cross-border e-commerce exports has increased more than 30%, which has driven a large number of SMEs to export. Cross-border e-commerce has been a new growth point of foreign trade. The total transaction scale of import and export by way of cross-border e-commerce in China reached RMB 9.1 trillion in 2018. In the context of global sluggish foreign trade and China's economic downturn, cross-border e-commerce undertakes the mission of promoting the transformation and upgrading of the open economy, improving the current development of the foreign trade industry and building new economic growth points.

2015年以来,跨境电商出口增速超过30%,带动了大量中小企业出口,成为新的外贸增长点。2018年中国进出口跨境电商整体交易规模达到9.1万亿元。全球外贸形势的低迷,中国经济下行的压力,使得跨境电商承担了推动开放型经济的转型升级,改善目前外贸行业的发展形势,打造新的经济增长点的任务。

(1) Promote the Transformation and Upgrading of China's Industrial Structure (促进我国产业结构转型升级)

As global economic growth weakens, traditional foreign trade and the volume of import and export trade grow slowly. The development of cross-border e-commerce directly promotes the advancement of modern service industries and related electronic information manufacturing industries such as logistics distribution, electronic payment, electronic certification, and other information services. Currently, there are more than 5,000 e-commerce platform enterprises in China. A group of local e-commerce platforms, international express, and third-party payment enterprises are rapidly emerging. More prominently, cross-border e-commerce will lead to changes in production modes and industrial organization. To meet the demand of diversification, multilevel and personalized overseas consumers, enterprises must focus on consumers, strengthen cooperation and innovation, as well as build a better service system. While improving product manufacturing process and quality, R&D (Research and Development) and brands need to be strengthened. Reconstruct value and industrial chain to maximize the allocation of resources and realize the transformation and upgrading of the industrial structure.

在全球经济增长放缓的大背景下,外贸发展情况普遍欠佳,进出口贸易交易额增长缓慢。跨境电子商务的发展,直接推动了物流配送、电子支付、电子认证、信息服务等现代服务业和相关电子信息制造业的发展。目前,我国电商平台企业已超过5000家,一批电商平台企业、物流快递、第三方支付本土企业快速崛起。更加突出的是,跨境电商将会引发生产方式、产业组织方式的变革。面对多样化、多层次、个性化的境外消费者需求,企业必须以消费者为中心,加强合作创新,构建完善的服务体系,在提升产品制造工艺、质量的同时,加强研发设计、品牌销售,重构价值链和产业链,最大限度地促进资源化配置,实现产业结构的转型升级。

(2) Help Enterprises to Create International Brands (有利于企业打造国际化品牌)

In the Internet age, brand and reputation are important components of enterprise competitiveness and the key factors in winning consumers. At present, the products and services of many companies in China are of good quality. But it is not known to foreign consumers. Cross-border e-commerce can effectively break channel monopoly, reduce intermediate links, shorten transaction time and save transaction costs, which can help enterprises create brands, enhance brand awareness, and move to the high value-added direction along the Smiling Curve. In particular, it has created a development space for some small and exquisite SMEs.

在互联网时代,品牌、口碑是企业竞争力的重要组成部分,也是赢得消费者青睐的关键因素。当前,我国许多企业的产品和服务质量很好,但不被外国消费者所知。而跨境电商能够有效打破渠道垄断,减少中间环节,缩短交易时间,节约交易成本,为我国企业创建品牌、提升品牌的知名度以及推动附加值沿微笑曲线向两端发展提供了有效的途径,尤其是给一些"小而美"的中小企业创造了发展空间。

(3) Speed up the Pace in Building China as a Strong Trader (加快我国建设贸易强国的步伐)

Cross-border e-commerce, being an emerging form of global foreign trade, features "no border" and "globalization". For enterprises, the open, multi-dimensional, stereoscopic and multilateral economic and trade cooperation mode built by cross-border e-commerce has significantly widened the channel for entering the international market. On the basis, cross-border e-commerce provides China a new way to cope with the new trade pattern without being marginalized. Cross-border e-commerce enterprises form an independent value chain system through the establishment of independent multinational production and sales network, which is conducive to both actively coping with the new global trade pattern and changing the situation that China has been persistently at the low value-added end on the Smiling Curve of the international trade chain. This will comprehensively enhance the transnational operating capacity and core competitiveness. Besides, it contributes to China's transformation from a large trading country to a strong trading power.

跨境电商作为全球外贸发展的新兴贸易形式,具有无边界、全球化的特征。对企业来说,跨境电商构建的开放、多维、立体的多边经贸合作模式,极大地拓宽了进入国际市场的路径,为我国应对贸易新格局,避免被边缘化提供了新途径。跨境电商企业,通过建立自主的跨国生产经营销售网络,形成自主价值链体系,有利于主动应对全球贸易新格局,也有利于改变长期以来我国在传统国际贸易分工格局中处于微笑曲线两端的局面,这将全面提升跨国经营能力与核心竞争力,为我国从贸易大国向贸易强国转变贡献力量。

(4) Promote the Co-Development of the Countries Along "the Belt and Road" (推动"一带一路"沿线国家经济共同发展)

As the world's longest economic cooperation belts and most promising economic corridor, "the Belt and Road" originates in China and runs through economic circles of Asia, Africa and Europe. It has a total population of approximately 4.4 billion and a total economic volume of about 21 trillion dollars. "the Belt and Road Initiative" plays an important role in the future development of China. And cross-border e-commerce plays a unique role in it. Chinese goods are sold to 54 countries along B&R such as Russia, Ukraine, Poland, Thailand, Egypt and Saudi Arabia through the e-commerce platform. Meanwhile, products from more than 50 countries along B&R have entered China through e-commerce platform. The link between private commerce and trade on the world map have become increasingly close through the "Online Silk Road", which further expands the circulation of culture and commodities, as well as helping achieve the goal of common prosperity between China and the countries along "the Belt and Road".

"一带一路"是世界上跨度最长的两条经济合作带,发端于中国,途径亚非欧经济圈,总人口约44亿,经济总量约21万亿美元,也是世界上最具发展潜力的经济大走廊。"一带一路"倡议在我国未来的发展中有着重要的地位,而跨境电商则在其中扮演着独一无二的角色。通过电商平台,中国商品销往俄罗斯、乌克兰、波兰、泰国、埃及、沙特阿拉伯等54个"一带一路"沿线国家。同时,超过50个"一带一路"沿线国家的商品通过电商平台走进了中国。通过"网上丝绸之路",民间商贸往来在世界地图上构成的连接线日益紧密,进一步扩大了文化、商品等的流通,实现了我国与"一带一路"沿线国家共同繁荣的目标。

## Section Four / Basic Qualities of Cross-Border E-Commerce Professional Talents
### 跨境电商专业人才素质

As a new format of "Internet + foreign trade", cross-border e-commerce has an irreplaceable strategic significance for promoting the transformation and upgrading of traditional foreign trade and manufacturing industries, as well as the development of cross-border trade of enterprises along the Belt and Road. Since 2015, China's cross-border e-commerce has grown at an average annual rate of more than 30%, while the cross-border e-commerce industry has a talent shortage of 4.5 million, and this gap has increased at a rate of 30% every year. The lack of professional talents is an important factor hindering the smooth development of cross-border e-commerce.

跨境电子商务作为"互联网+外贸"的新业态,对促进传统外贸和制造业转型升级、服务"一带一路"沿线企业跨境贸易发展具有不可替代的重大战略意义。2015年以来,我国跨境电子商务以年均超过30%的增速迅猛发展,而跨境电商行业人才缺口达450万人,并且这个缺口以每年30%的增速扩大。跨境电商专业人才的缺乏是阻碍跨境电商行业顺利发展的重要因素。

Cross-border e-commerce industry needs a large number of complex talents and professional and technical talents, which are quite different from traditional trade and e-commerce talents. There is a broad coverage of cross-border e-commerce positions including procurement specialists, operations specialists, customs specialists, logistics specialists, customer service specialists and so on. What are the basic qualities of a qualified cross-border e-commerce professional talent?

跨境电商行业需要大量复合型人才和专业技术型人才,与传统贸易、电子商务人才有较大差异。跨境电商主要岗位包括采购专员、运营专员、报关专员、物流专员、客服专员等,涉及面广。那么,一名合格的跨境电商专业人才需要具备哪些基本素质呢?

(1) Professional Ethics (职业道德)

Professional ethics refers to the ethical requirements and corresponding codes of conduct that must be observed in the actual occupational activities of people engaged in certain occupations. It is the sum of moral norms and ethics that are related to professional activities and are in line with their own professional characteristics. Professional ethics includes dedication, honesty and trustworthiness, law-abiding attitude, seriousness and responsibility, team spirit, as well as the sense of social responsibility and participation. In any field, professional ethics is the foundation of success. Cross-border e-commerce practitioners must constantly improve their own quality and self-cultivation, strictly regulate their own behaviors at work, discover and change bad work habits in a timely manner. Whether it is in cross-border e-commerce industry or other fields, only by focusing on professional ethics can you achieve excellent results.

职业道德,指从事一定职业的人在实际的职业活动当中应该遵守的具有一定职业特征的道德要求和相应的行为准则,是与职业活动相互联系的符合自身职业特征的道德准则和道德规范的总和。职业道德包括爱岗敬业、诚实守信、遵纪守法、认真负责、团结合作,具有社会责任感和参与意识等。无论在什么领域,职业道德都是成功之本。跨境电商从业人员必须不断提高自身的素质和修养,在工作中严格规范自己的各项行为,及时发现并改正不良的工作习惯。不论是跨境电商行业还是其他领域,只有讲求职业道德,才能取得优异的成绩。

(2) Foreign Language Communication Skills (外语沟通能力)

Good online foreign language communication skills are critical to the success of cross-border e-commerce. Foreign language communication ability of cross-border e-commerce is mainly reflected in customer service and after-sales service, including delivery notice, receipt confirmation, customer return, customer satisfaction review and so on. It is also important to have the ability to accurately listen to customers' opinions and express information. It can improve shop ratings, customer satisfaction and increase customer stickiness. According to statistics, Central Asia, South Asia, West Asia and other regions covered by "the Belt and Road" involve more than 40 official languages. Therefore, the ability to communicate in minor languages is also crucial to the development of the markets of countries along "the Belt and Road".

良好的线上外语沟通能力对于跨境电商的成功十分关键。跨境电商中的外语沟通能力主要体现在客服和售后服务方面,包括发货通知、收货确认、客户退换货、客户满意度评价等。良好的外语沟通能力体现在准确听取客户的意见和表达信息的能力,对于提升店铺评分具有促进作用,可以提高客户的消费满意度,增加客户黏性。据统计,"一带一路"所覆盖的中亚、南亚、西亚等地区,涉及官方语言达40余种。因此,具备小语种语言的沟通能力对于开拓"一带一路"沿线国家市场也至关重要。

(3) Operational Capability of Cross-Border E-Commerce Platform (跨境电商平台运营能力)

The operation of cross-border e-commerce platform includes product description, page optimization, off-site marketing, supply chain management, data analysis, after-sales customer service and many other aspects of the operation of international e-commerce platforms such as Amazon, eBay, Wish. It requires cross-border e-commerce talents to be familiar with the operation rules and contents of the network platform, help stores realize the increase of transaction per customer, sales volume, profit and customer satisfaction. All these require cross-border e-commerce talents to have some practical experience, management analysis ability and innovative thinking ability.

跨境电商平台运营工作包括在亚马逊、易贝、Wish等国际电商平台进行产品描述、页面优化、站外营销推广、供应链管理、数据分析、售后客服等很多方面的运营工作。这要求跨境电商人才熟悉网络平台操作规则和操作内容,能够帮助店铺实现消费者客单价加大、店铺销售额增加、店铺利润额上升和顾客满意度提升等。这些都要求跨境电商人才有一定的实操经验、管理分析能力和创新性思维能力。

(4) International Vision (国际化视野)

Under the background of economic globalization, cross-border e-commerce talents must have international vision, global mind, and carry out cross-border e-commerce marketing, brand building and international customer service activities according to local conditions. Cross-border e-commerce talents need to understand the cultural traditions, consumption habits, dietary habits, religious customs, legal systems and other information of the country where consumers live, which is conducive to product selection, market positioning and marketing activities. In the process of cross-border e-commerce, domestic enterprises especially need talents with knowledge of international taxation, intellectual property and trademark protection to avoid infringement and huge fines.

在经济全球化的背景下,跨境电商人才必须具有国际化视野,胸怀全球,因地制宜地进行跨境电商营销、品牌建设以及国际客户服务等活动。跨境电商人才需要理解消费者所在国的文化传统、消费习惯、饮食习惯、宗教习俗、法律制度等信息,这有利于选品,进行市场定位和营销活动等。国内企业在从事跨境电商的过程中,尤其需要懂国际税务、知识产权、商标保护方面知识的人才,以避免侵权和巨额罚款等问题。

(5) Lifelong Learning (终身学习能力)

Lifelong Education was first proposed by Parl Lengrand, Director-General of UNESCO Adult Education Bureau, during the International Conference on Adult Education Promotion held in 1965 under the auspices of UNESCO. Lifelong learning refers to the continuous learning process for every member of society in order to meet the needs of social development and individual development. Lifelong learning can enable us to overcome difficulties and solve new problems in our work, meet our needs for survival and development, enable us to get more space for development and better realize our own values, as well as enrich our spiritual life and constantly improve the quality of life. To become qualified cross-border e-commerce talents, we should have a deep understanding of lifelong learning, and put the concept of lifelong learning into action.

"终身教育"最早于1965年在联合国教科文组织主持召开的成人教育促进国际会议期间,由联合国教科文组织成人教育局局长保罗·朗格朗正式提出。终身学习是指社会每个成员为适应社会发展和实现个体发展的需要,贯穿于人的一生的、持续的学习过程。终身学习能使我们克服工作中的困难,解决工作中的新问题;能满足我们生存和发展的需要;能使我们得到更大的发展空间,更好地实现自身价值;能充实我们的精神生活,不断提高生活品质。想要成为一名合格的跨境电商人才,更应该深刻理解终身学习,并付诸行动,树立起终身学习的理念。

## Section Five / Extensive Reading: Successful Cases of Cross-Border E-Commerce

### 拓展阅读:跨境电商成功案例

There are many small and medium-sized sellers on AliExpress. There is no independent production line and no much investment. Ms. Huang is one of them. She is from Lishui, Zhejiang Province, and is currently focusing on selling evening bags. In 2015, 5,000 evening bags were sent from her shop and delivered to more than 10 European and North American countries through international parcels.

全球速卖通上有大量中小卖家,没有独立的生产线,投入不多,黄女士就是其中一员。她来自浙江丽水,目前专注于销售晚宴包。2015年,5000个晚宴包从她的店铺里发出,通过国际包裹运送到10余个欧美国家。

After graduating from college, Ms. Huang began working with her husband on foreign trade in the clothing market. After several years of understanding the clothing industry, they came up with the idea of opening their own online store. In 2012, Ms. Huang and her husband opened the first AliExpress store, mainly for women's wear, all of which came from 1688.com. They put the selected products on their own store. If someone orders, they will purchase the product on 1688.com. The products will be sent to their home first. After a certain amount, these products will be packaged and sent to the shipping company for delivery. After several years of operation, Ms. Huang found that among foreign customers, Russian customers like low prices and discounts best, and European and American ones are most concerned about customer evaluation. Compared with domestic customers, foreign customers have more patience with the arrival time.

大学毕业以后,黄女士就开始和丈夫一起从事外贸服装工作。通过几年对服装行业的了解,他们萌生了自己开网店的想法。2012年,黄女士和她的丈夫开了第一家速卖通店铺,以经营女装为主,货源全部来自阿里巴巴1688网。他们把选中的商品上架到自己的店铺上,如果有人下单,他们就到1688上购买,产品会先寄到家,累积到一定量以后打包寄给代运公司统一寄出。经过几年的经营,黄女士发现在国外客户中,俄罗斯客户最喜欢低价和折扣商品,欧美客户最在意客户评价。而相对于国内客户,国外客户对商品的到货时间有更多耐心。

However, in 2014, due to the increasing number of women's wear sellers on AliExpress, the competition became increasingly fierce. The business of Ms. Huang's women's clothing store was stable and lacked growth. Ms. Huang was looking for ways to develop her own store. She found that the products of AliExpress were not limited to one single category, so she can expand other categories to increase sales. Through platform data analysis and market research, Ms. Huang decided to increase the category of evening bags. Although evening bag was still not popular in China, it had a good market in Europe and North America. It was a relatively narrow category under luggage, with novel and unique styles. At that time, the competition on the platform was not too intense. So Ms. Huang opened her second AliExpress store, focusing on evening bags, and began to think about how to carry out refined operations.

但在2014年,由于速卖通上的女装卖家越来越多,竞争日益激烈,黄女士的女装店的生意趋于平稳,缺少增长点。黄女士到处寻觅方法来发展自己的店铺,她发现速卖通店铺的产品不限制单一品类，可以扩充其他类目来增加销售额。通过平台数据分析和市场调研，黄女士决定增加晚宴包这一品类。虽然晚宴包在中国还不太流行，在欧美国家却有不错的市场，是箱包类目中较为细分的一个类目，其款式追求新颖独特，当时在平台上竞争也不太激烈。于是，黄女士当年就开了第二家速卖通店铺，专营晚宴包，并开始思考如何进行精细化运营。

Beginning in January 2016, AliExpress officially implemented the single-store single-category operation rule and charged the merchants for management. Most domestic small and medium sellers rely on the 1688 model, and multi-category operations are very common. In the absence of a supply chain and brand advantage, single-category operations mean discarding most customers. After in-depth observation, Ms. Huang concluded that evening bag is a relatively narrow category, but it is very popular in Europe and North America, and the competition is not intense. Thus, she decided to turn off the women's clothing store that had accumulated 3 diamonds and kept the evening bag store.

自2016年1月开始，速卖通店铺正式执行单店铺单类目运营规则，并对商家进行收费管理。国内中小卖家大多依赖1688拿货的模式，多类目经营非常常见。在没有供应链和品牌优势的前提下，单品类经营意味着舍弃大部分客户。黄女士在深入观察后得出结论，晚宴包是一个相对小众的二级类目，但在欧美地区非常受欢迎，而且竞争也不算激烈。于是，她决定关掉已经积攒了3颗钻的女装店，保留了晚宴包店铺。

In the process of operating the evening bag store, firstly, Ms. Huang insisted on the way of uploading one product per time. If this product has the potential to become a hot sale product, she will take pictures by herself to ensure that the style of picture and product is unified. Many agents use the data package to upload products with one step, and sometimes 500 new products can be added in one day. Although more products will have more exposures, the data package will cause the shop pictures to be inconsistent, the number of products is confusing, and the homepage picture is disorganized. Secondly, Ms. Huang classifies the 500 evening bags in the store according to materials, colors, etc., so that customers can search accurately, while most luggage stores will use automatic classification, and all evening bags are grouped into one category. Finally, the pricing is reasonable. Take the new satin bag as an example, Ms. Huang will search for the price of the competing product before uploading, usually setting the price at a reasonable price between the lowest and the highest price.

黄女士在经营晚宴包店铺的过程中,首先坚持单个产品上新的方式。如果是有潜力成为爆品的商品,她还会自己拍图上新,保证图片和产品风格统一。很多代理商是用数据包一步上新的,有些一天可以上新500个产品。虽然产品种类多、曝光多,但数据包会造成店铺图片不统一,产品数量混乱,首页图杂乱无章。其次,黄女士把店里的500个晚宴包按照材质、颜色等进行分类,方便客户精准搜索。而大多数综合类包店会使用自动分类的方式,所有晚宴包都归在一个类目里。最后,合理定价。比如在上一个新款绸缎包之前,黄女士会先搜索竞品价格,然后通常会把价格设定为最低价和最高价之间的一个合理价格。

Adapted from www.cifnews.com (改编自雨果网)

# Chapter Two
## Trading Platforms of Cross-Border E-Commerce

# 跨境电商
# 运营平台

## Lead-in
## 导入

The prosperity and development of cross-border e-commerce industry is inseparable from cross-border e-commerce trading platforms. With these platforms, enterprises can easily get started, open stores on the platform, and upload products. They don't need to establish or maintain their own websites, neither do they need to promote their own sites. With the brand effect of these trading platforms, enterprises can obtain a large amount of traffic and orders, which can effectively save operating costs for enterprises and obtain considerable profits in the short term. At present, there are many cross-border e-commerce platforms in China. This chapter will introduce the characteristics and basic operations of AliExpress, Amazon, Wish and eBay respectively, four main cross-border e-commerce trading platforms in the world.

跨境电商产业的繁荣发展离不开跨境电商运营平台。借助平台进行跨境电商经营活动,企业可以轻松入门,在平台上开设店铺,上传产品信息即可,不需要自己建立站点进行维护,也不需要自己做站点推广。企业借助平台本身的品牌效应就能获得大量流量和订单,有效地为企业节约经营成本,在短期内获得可观的收益。目前我国跨境电商平台众多,本章会依次介绍速卖通、亚马逊、Wish和易贝四大跨境电商运营平台的特点及基本操作。

## Section One / **AliExpress**
## 速卖通

### 1. Characteristics of AliExpress (速卖通平台的特点)

AliExpress was officially launched in April 2010, also known as the "international version of Taobao" (shown in Figure 2-1). AliExpress is an online trading platform by Alibaba that integrates orders, payment and logistics to help SMEs contact terminal wholesale retailers, sell in small and multiple batches, and expand profit margins.

全球速卖通于2010年4月正式上线,被广大卖家称为"国际版淘宝"(见图2-1)。速卖通是阿里巴巴旗下让中小企业接触终端批发零售商，小批量多批次快速销售，拓展利润空间而全力打造的融合订单、支付、物流于一体的外贸在线交易平台。

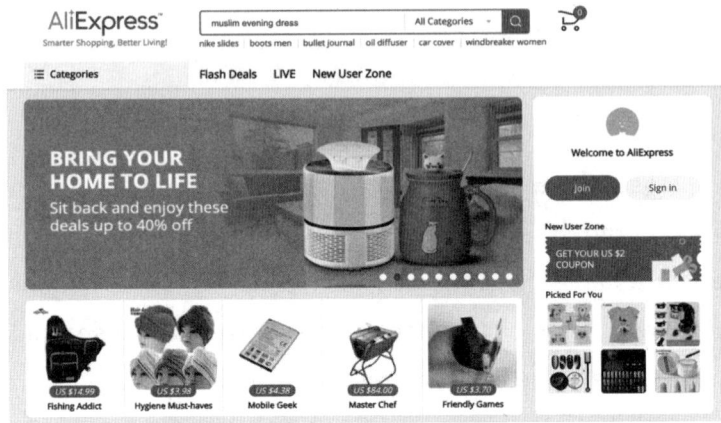

Figure 2-1（图2-1）

At the beginning of AliExpress, Alibaba acquired the US e-commerce SaaS provider Vendio, which quickly opened the American Online retail market for AliExpress. In terms of logistics, Alibaba has formed a strategic alliance with international logistics giant UPS, although most users will choose a more cost-effective logistic, this provides users with a high-end logistic option. In terms of funding, Alibaba's cooperation with the world's largest online payment company PayPal, although only lasted for one year, has improved the order conversion rate of AliExpress during the initial period.

速卖通诞生初期，阿里巴巴全资收购了美国电子商务 SaaS 提供商 Vendio 公司，为速卖通迅速打开美国在线零售市场。在物流方面，阿里巴巴与国际物流巨头 UPS 结成战略联盟，尽管大多数用户会选择性价比更高的物流，但这为用户提供了一种高端的物流选择。在资金方面，阿里巴巴与全球最大的在线支付公司 PayPal 合作，虽然仅维持了一年时间，但在初期极大地提高了速卖通的订单转化率。

After several years of development, the current transaction volume of the platform reaches an average annual growth rate of 400%. The top trading countries are Russia, United States, Brazil, Spain, Britain, France, Canada, Australia, Israel, Ukraine and so on. As of April 2017, the buyers of AliExpress have covered more than 220 countries and regions. It covers clothing, 3C, home, jewelry and other 26 categories of products. Overseas buyers exceeded 100 million, with the average daily visitors exceeding 20 million. In May 2017, Alibaba announced that AliExpress has covered all countries and regions along "the Belt and Road". As of 2018, 56% of the buyers on the AliExpress platform came from countries and regions along "the Belt and Road", and these consumers contributed 57% of the orders and 49% of the transaction volume of the AliExpress platform. AliExpress has ushered in a period of rapid development in the past year. Not only in the traditional strong market, Russia continues to be the largest e-commerce platform, and continues to grow in developed markets such as Spain and France, and has seen strong growth in the "the Belt and the Road" emerging markets in Eastern Europe, the Middle East, Africa, etc. According to the data of July 29, 2019, AliExpress is ranked 35th on the Alexa global website.

经过数年的发展,该平台的交易额以平均每年400%的速度增长,排名靠前的交易国家有俄罗斯、美国、巴西、西班牙、英国、法国、加拿大、澳大利亚、以色列、乌克兰等。截至2017年4月,全球速卖通已经覆盖220多个国家和地区的买家;覆盖服装服饰、3C产品、家居、饰品等共30个一级行业类目;海外买家突破1亿,平均每日访客超2000万。2017年5月,阿里巴巴对外宣布,其旗下的全球速卖通已覆盖"一带一路"沿线全部国家和地区。截至2018年,速卖通平台上56%的买家来自"一带一路"沿线国家和地区,这些消费者贡献了速卖通平台57%的订单量和49%的交易金额。速卖通在过去一年迎来高速发展期。不仅在传统强势市场俄罗斯继续稳列第一大电商平台,在西班牙、法国等欧洲发达市场保持持续增长,并且在东欧、中东、非洲等"一带一路"新兴市场呈现出强劲的增长势头。根据2019年7月29日的数据,速卖通在Alexa全球网站排第35位。

(1) Advantage of AliExpress（平台优势）

With the popularity of Alibaba International Station, coupled with the promotion of related sites from other continents, Google online promotion and other channels, AliExpress wins a steady stream of high-quality flow with global buyer resources, and the App downloads rank the first among more than 100 countries. Compared with other competitors, AliExpress also has a clear advantage in terms of platform transaction fee rate, commission rates as low as 5%–8%. AliExpress also enjoys a wealth of Taobao merchandise resources. Its Taobao sales function makes it very convenient for sellers to sell Taobao products to the world. AliExpress also provides one-stop service of products translation, products releasing, payment, logistics and other services. Moreover, AliExpress platform provides a complete website integrity and security system to protect the transaction process and avoid fraud.

凭借阿里巴巴国际站的知名度,以及各大洲相关联盟站点、谷歌线上推广等渠道为速卖通引入源源不断的优质流量,速卖通拥有覆盖全球的买家资源,应用下载量在100多个国家排第一。和其他竞争对手相比,速卖通在平台交易手续费率上也有明显的优势,佣金费率低至5%—8%。速卖通还享有丰富的淘宝商品资源,其淘代销功能使得卖家可非常方便地将淘宝商品一键卖向全球,速卖通为卖家提供一站式商品翻译、上架、支付、物流等服务。而且,速卖通平台提供完善的网站诚信安全体系,为交易过程保驾护航,避免货款受骗。

In addition, AliExpress sellers have the opportunity to enjoy the right of becoming "good sellers in China". The benefits include traffic support, marketing resources, brand protection, grievance protection, early lending, service upgrades, etc.

除此之外,速卖通卖家还有机会享受"中国好卖家"权益,包括流量支持、营销资源、品牌保护、申诉保障、提前放款和服务升级等。

(2) Marketable Products（适销产品）

First of all, the products should be suitable for delivery through air express delivery. These products should basically meet the following conditions: relatively small and could be delivered by express with low international logistic costs; high added value, not suitable for single sales if product value is less than shipping, but still suitable to be packed for sale; lower logistic costs; unique, in order to continuously stimulate buyers to purchase and have high online transactions volume; reasonable price, if online prices are higher than local market prices, they cannot attract buyers to order online. According to the above conditions, marketable products for AliExpress mainly include clothing, beauty & health, jewelry & watches, lights, consumer electronics, computer & office, phones & accessories, parts of automobiles & motorcycles, handicrafts, sports & outdoors and so on.

首先要有适宜通过航空快递运输的商品。这些商品基本符合下面的条件:体积较小,主要是方便以快递方式运输,降低国际物流成本;附加值较高,价值低过运费的单件商品不适合单件销售,可以打包出售;降低物流成本占比;具备独特性,在线交易业绩佳的商品需要独具特色,才能不断刺激买家的购买欲望;价格较合理,在线交易价格若高于产品在当地的市场价,就无法吸引买家在线下单。根据以上的条件,适宜在全球速卖通销售的商品主要包括服饰、美容健康、珠宝手表、灯具、消费性电子产品、电脑和办公用品、手机和配件、汽车和摩托车配件、工艺品、体育与户外用品等。

Sellers can use AliExpress's own "analytics" feature to guide shop selections. By looking at the global dimension of national heat analysis, segmentation of buyer market analysis, commodity analysis, etc., sellers can better understand global market conditions and trends, and choose or produce marketable products based on buyer's demand.

卖家可以使用速卖通自有的"数据纵横"功能为店铺选品提供指导。卖家可以通过查看全球维度的国家热度分析、细分买家市场分析、商品分析等,更好地了解全球市场行情及趋势,选择或根据买方需求生产出适销对路的产品。

## 2. Registration（店铺注册）

Step 1: Go to https://www.aliexpress.com/ and click "Chinese Seller Registration" or "Non-Chinese Seller Registration" under the "Seller Center", as shown in Figure 2-2.

步骤一:进入 https://www.aliexpress.com/,点击"卖家中心"下的"中国卖家入驻"或"非中国卖家入驻",如图 2-2 所示。

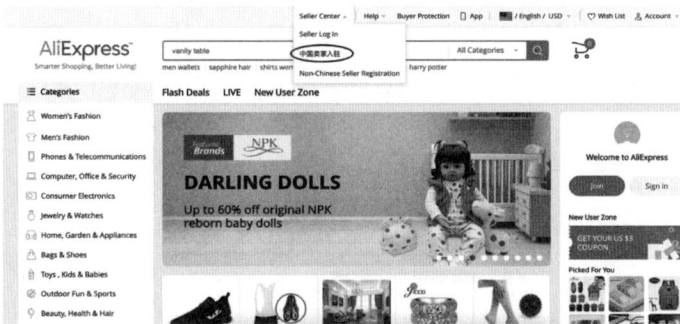

Figure 2-2（图2-2）

Step 2: Let us take the "Chinese Seller Registration" as an example. After clicking "Register", the interface is shown as Figure 2-3.

步骤二:我们以"中国卖家入驻"为例,点击"注册"之后,即进入如图 2-3 所示的界面。

Figure 2-3（图2-3）

Step 3: As shown in Figure 2-4, enter the email address, check the two membership agreements and services, register, and then log in to the email address to confirm the registration. Then, as shown in Figure 2-5, after completing the account information, the registration is completed.

步骤三：如图2-4所示，输入电子邮箱，勾选同意以下两项会员协议及服务，并进行注册，然后登录电子邮箱确认注册。再按照图2-5所示，填写完成账号信息之后，即完成注册。

① 设置用户名　　② 填写账号信息　　✔ 注册成功

电子邮箱　　请输入邮箱

验证　　》　请按住滑块，拖动到最右边

☐ 创建网站账号的同时，我同意：
- 遵守Aliexpress.com 会员协议
- 愿意接收相关来自Aliexpress.com的会员及服务邮件

下一步

Figure 2-4（图2-4）

① 设置用户名　　② 填写账号信息　　✔ 注册成功

登录名　　▬▬▬▬▬

请设置登录密码

登录密码　　设置你的登录密码

密码确认　　请再次输入你的密码

英文姓名　　名　　姓

手机号码　　请输入手机号码

联系地址　　-- 请选择省 -- ⬍　-- 请选择市 -- ⬍　-- 请选择县城 -- ⬍

在线经验：　☐ 天猫　☐ 亚马逊　☐ ebay　☐ 1688
　　　　　　☐ 阿里巴巴国际站　☐ wish　☐ 无
　　　　　　☐ 其他

Figure 2-5（图2-5）

Step 4: After the registration is completed, start AliExpress real-name authentication, as shown in Figure 2-6. Select corporate account or self-employed for certification, and you need to prepare the business license, corporate identity card and other materials in advance, as shown in Figure 2-7.

步骤四:注册成功之后,进行速卖通实名认证,见图2-6所示。选择企业账户或者个体户进行认证,需要提前准备好企业营业执照、法人身份证等材料,如图2-7所示。

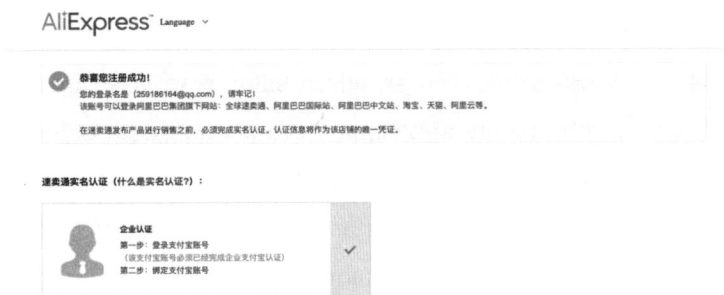

Figure 2-6 (图2-6)

Figure 2-7 (图2-7)

## 3. AliExpress Platform Analysis (速卖通平台解析)

After completing the store registration and authentication, the seller needs to select a category according to the products they sell, apply for the trademark certification and secondary category certification afterwards, and finally pay for the corresponding annual technical service fee according to the selected category. Basically, it is RMB10,000 per year, and certain categories will charge higher. The annual fee is charged according to business categories, and it is required to be paid separately for different business categories. Under the same business category, the annual fee is paid only once.

完成店铺注册及认证之后,卖家需要根据经营的产品选择大类,确定大类之后进行商标认证,通过之后进行二级类目的认证,最后根据选择的类目缴纳相应的技术服务年费,基本上费用为一万元一年,个别类目会高一点。年费按照经营大类收取,入驻不同经营大类需分别缴纳年费。同一经营大类下,年费只需缴纳一份。

Currently, AliExpress is divided into basic sales plan and standard sales plan. The basic sales plan has certain functional limitations, including the number of products released, open categories and exposures. However, in terms of annual fee settlement, as long as the account is not closed because of violation of rules, the annual fee will be refunded in full. The standard sales plan is an upgraded version of the basic sales plan, which is only applicable to business users. If it is operated by the end of the year, the unused annual fee can be returned. The seller of the basic sales plan can subsequently upgrade to standard sales plan after satisfying certain conditions, but the seller who chooses standard sales plan cannot switch to basic sales plan within a natural year.

目前,速卖通分为基础销售计划和标准销售计划。基础销售计划在功能上有一定的限制,包括发布的产品数量、开放的类目和曝光量等。但在年费结算上,只要不因违规违约而被关闭账号,最终都能全额返还年费。而标准销售计划则为基础销售计划的升级版,仅适用于企业用户,如果经营到年底,可返还未使用的年费。基础销售计划的卖家在满足一定条件后,可后续自主升级为标准销售计划,但标准销售计划的卖家在一个自然年内不可切换至基础销售计划。

After completing the above series of work, seller can enter and make use of AliExpress dashboard. AliExpress dashboard consists of six main modules: Products, Orders, Store, Marketing, Analytics, and Violations, as shown in Figure 2-8. After the seller pass the review of AliExpress platform, the products can be released to the account. The detailed way is to click "My Dashboard" tab at the top of the background, and then click "Publish Product" in the left portal for product release. For the released products, you can also click "Manage Products" button for effective management, where you can modify, query, delete and use other corresponding functions.

完成上述一系列工作之后,卖家可以进入速卖通后台进行操作。速卖通后台包含商品、交易、店铺、营销活动、数据纵横以及违规6个主要模块,如图2-8所示。卖家通过速卖通平台的审核后,可以进入账号后台进行产品发布,具体方法为点击后台上方的"我的速卖通"选项卡,之后就可以点击左侧快速入口中的"发布产品"按钮进行产品发布。对于已发布的产品,还可以点击"管理产品"按钮进行有效管理,在这里可以对产品信息进行修改、查询、删除等对应的操作。

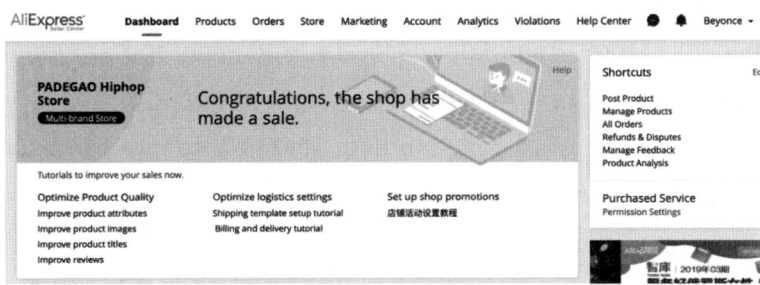

Figure 2-8 (图2-8)

The order module includes all order information, logistic options, capital accounts and evaluation management, as shown in Figure 2-9. Through the order module, the seller can view the order and select the appropriate shipping method for delivery, or export the order in bulk. During the transaction process, buyers and sellers can communicate effectively through the online international version of Alitalk, in-station message, order message and email, etc.

交易模块包括所有订单信息、物流选择、资金账户和评价管理等,如图2-9所示。卖家通过交易模块可以查看订单并选择合适的快递进行发货,也可以批量导出订单。买卖双方在交易过程中,可以通过线上国际版阿里旺旺、站内信、订单留言和电子邮箱信息等渠道进行有效沟通。

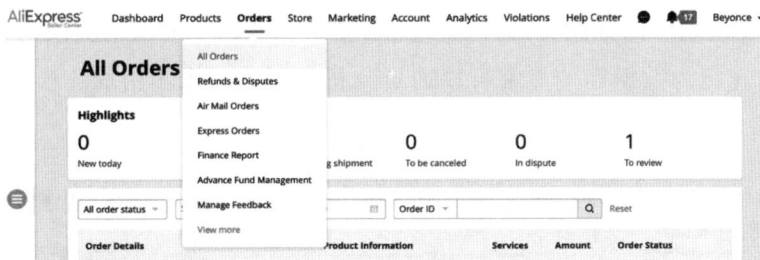

Figure 2-9 (图2-9)

In store module, the seller can manage the store. Sellers who enter as enterprises can choose the appropriate type from official store, exlcusive agency and franchised store. Sellers can also decorate stores and add brand stories to enhance brand image and buyer sentiment.

在店铺模块,卖家可以进行店铺管理。以企业身份入驻的卖家可以从官方店、专卖店和专营店三种店铺类型中选择合适的类型进行经营。卖家还可以装修店铺,添加品牌故事,以提升品牌形象和买家好感度。

The promotional activities of AliExpress platform are mainly divided into Platform Promotions, Store Promotions, Affiliate Marketing and Targeted Advertising. When buyers search for a keyword or go through category to search results page, they will see the results of natural sorting, and marketing campaigns can help sellers improve the ranking of the product in AliExpress order, helping sellers achieve multi-channel traffic.

速卖通平台的推广活动主要分为平台活动、店铺活动、联盟营销和精准广告。当买家通过搜索某个关键词或通过类目来到搜索结果页面时,会看到自然排序的结果,而营销推广活动可以帮助卖家提高该产品在速卖通排序中的排名,帮助卖家实现多渠道引流。

The analytics module includes Real Time Data Report, Traffic Analysis, Store Performance Analysis, Product Analysis, Optimization Tools, Market Information, etc. It is a data analysis product based on massive data of the platform. The data can provide guidance to the seller for store marketing, as shown in Figure 2-10. Sellers can view 24 hour real-time updates of data, including exposure, browsing, visitors, visitor behavior data, and the like. Sellers can analyze the data and select time to use targeted advertising, monitor store and platform activity, explore potential products, and create hot sale.

数据纵横模块包含实时风暴、流量分析、经营分析、商品分析、优化工具、市场行情等内容,是基于平台海量数据打造的一款数据分析产品,卖家可以根据数据纵横提供的数据,为店铺营销提供指导,如图2-10所示。卖家可以查看24小时实时更新的数据,含曝光、浏览、访客、访客行为数据等。卖家可以通过分析数据选时操作精准广告、监控店铺及平台活动效果、发掘潜力产品、打造爆品。

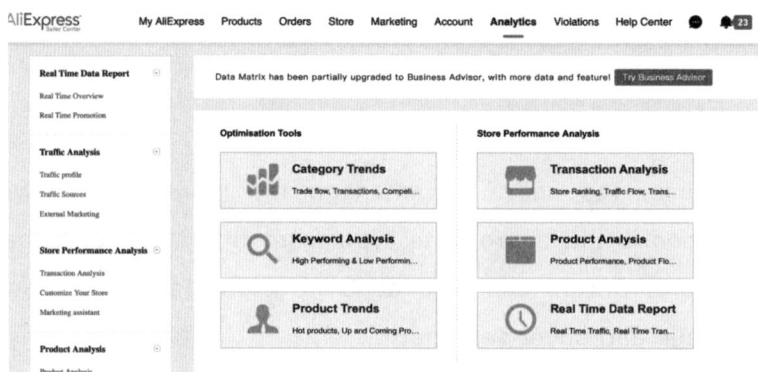

Figure 2-10 (图2-10)

The violations module includes violations of product quality, infringements of intellectual property rights and prohibited products, trade rules and others. If there is any infringement of intellectual property rights, you only have one chance to make an appeal; if fails, your account will possibly be terminated. If infringements of intellectual property rights and trade rules and other forms of violations reach 48 points, your right to operate will be terminated. If violations of product information quality reach 12 points, the account will be frozen for 7 days. The three sets of points will be deducted and accumulated separately, and the penalty will be executed separately.

违规模块包括商品信息质量违规、知识产权禁限售违规、交易违规等。知识产权严重侵权案件只有一次申诉机会,申诉不成功可能会被直接关闭账号。知识产权禁限售违规、交易违规及其他违规积分满48分,店铺将被关闭;商品信息质量违规积分满12分,账号将被冻结7天;三套积分制分别扣分,积分分别累计,处罚分别执行。

# Section Two / **Amazon**
## 亚马逊

## 1. Characteristics of Amazon (亚马逊平台的特点)

Founded in 1995 and headquartered in Seattle, USA, Amazon is the largest online e-commerce company in the United States. At the beginning, Amazon only sold books, and after continuous investment and acquisition, it has become the world's largest online retailer and the second largest Internet company in the world. Amazon platform offers millions of unique new, refurbished and second-hand products, including books, electronics, household items, toys, baby products, food, apparel, health and personal care products, sports and outdoor products, etc. Amazon's official website is shown in Figure 2-11.

亚马逊公司成立于1995年,总部位于美国西雅图,是美国最大的一家网络电子商务公司。刚开始亚马逊只销售书籍,经过不断的投资与收购,它已成为全球商品品种最多的网上零售商和全球第二大互联网企业。亚马逊平台为客户提供数百万种独特的全新、翻新及二手商品,包括图书、电子产品、家居用品、玩具、婴幼儿用品、食品、服饰、健康和个人护理用品、体育及户外用品等。图2-11为亚马逊美国站官网。

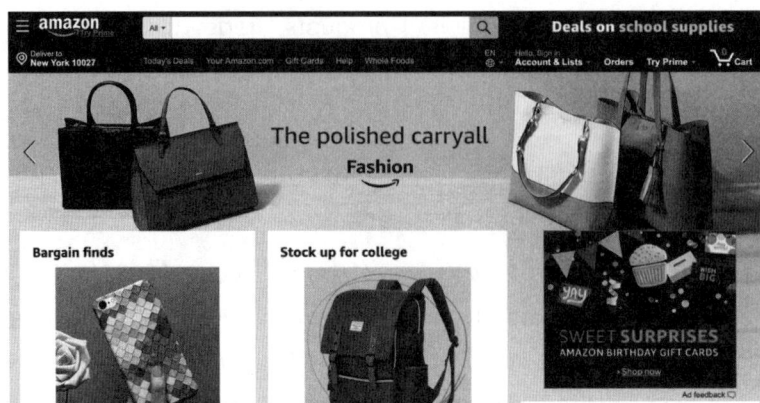

Figure 2-11 (图2-11)

Amazon China's predecessor was Joyo, founded in 2000, it was acquired by Amazon in 2004 and is headquartered in Beijing. Amazon China mainly operates 32 major categories of books, audio & video, clothing & luggage, mobile & digital products, etc. It has a leading position in China's online retail market. Amazon China adheres to the "customer-centered" philosophy and is committed to creating a reliable online shopping environment for consumers in terms of low prices, product selection and convenience. In 2016, Amazon introduced the successful Prime membership service to China. On April 18, 2019, Amazon notified Chinese sellers that it would no longer operate China's domestic market business and stop providing services to merchants from July 18. Amazon China plans to close the distribution center within 90 days, gradually reducing support for Chinese domestic merchants, and only retaining Kindle and cross-border trade services.

亚马逊中国的前身是卓越网,创立于2000年,2004年被亚马逊公司收购,总部位于北京。亚马逊中国主要经营图书音像、服装箱包、手机数码等32个大类的产品,在中国的网上零售业具有领先地位。亚马逊中国坚持"以客户为中心"的理念,致力于从低价、选品、便利三个方面为消费者打造一个可信赖的网上购物环境。2016年,亚马逊将在美国取得成功的Prime会员服务引入中国。2019年4月18日,亚马逊通知中国卖家,从7月18日起将不再运营中国国内市场业务并停止向商户提供服务。亚马逊中国计划在90天内关闭配送中心,逐步减少对中国内销商户的支持,仅保留Kindle和跨境贸易。

Before 2012, if Chinese sellers wanted to settle in Amazon US site, they could only register as US citizens. Since 2012, Amazon has established a professional team of Amazon Global Selling in China, and it is committed to bringing excellent Chinese enterprises to Amazon platform to sell products directly to overseas consumers.

After several years of hard work, the major Amazon sites, Canada, Germany, Britain, France, Italy, Spain, Japan, Mexico, Australia, India and China, have been fully opened to Chinese sellers. More than 140 multiple operation centers help Chinese sellers sell their products to more than 180 countries and regions around the world.

2012年之前,中国卖家想要入驻亚马逊美国站,只能以美国公民的身份注册账号。从2012年开始,亚马逊在中国组建了"全球开店"项目的专业团队,致力于把优秀的中国企业引入到亚马逊平台销售产品,直接面对海外消费者。经过几年的努力,目前亚马逊美国、加拿大、德国、英国、法国、意大利、西班牙、日本、墨西哥、澳大利亚、印度这些主要的站点已向中国卖家全面开放,有遍布全球的140多个运营中心帮助中国卖家将产品销往世界180多个国家和地区。

Compared to other cross-border e-commerce platforms, Amazon has the following characteristics.

相较于其他跨境电商平台,亚马逊有以下几项特点。

(1) A unique evaluation system. Amazon's evaluation system includes review and feedback. Review is about consumer evaluation about product quality. The page displays the number of reviews, star ratings, and review contents. If they are all 5 stars and the review content is good, you can buy them with confidence. If you see a lot of 1 star, 2 stars negative reviews, it is very likely that many overseas buyers will directly close the page and choose other similar products. Feedback is the final rating about the seller's logistic and after-sales service. It is one of the most important features of Amazon, which is different from other platforms. It also shows that Amazon attaches great importance to the buyer's shopping experience.

独特的评价体系。亚马逊的评价体系包括评论和反馈。评论是消费者针对产品质量的评价,页面会显示评价数量、星级评分和评价内容。如果都是5星好评,评价内容也不错,就可以放心购买。如果看到有不少1星、2星的差评,估计很多海外买家会直接关掉页面,选择其他同类产品。反馈是关于卖家物流和售后服务的最终评级,是亚马逊区别于其他平台的最主要特征之一,这也说明亚马逊非常重视买家的购物体验。

(2) Emphasize on products rather than stores. Most e-commerce platforms are generally shop-centered, but Amazon emphasizes on products, and does not have the concept of store. Amazon does not open a special second-level domain name for the store, and does not rate stores. Buyers search for products on Amazon and directly go into the product description page. They will not remember the seller's store name. The seller can save a lot of time and effort on logistics and after-sales

service by using the unified product description page provided by the platform. This mode is perfect for promoting a single item.

重产品轻店铺。大多数电商平台一般都以店铺为中心，但亚马逊强调以产品为中心，没有店铺的概念。亚马逊不为店铺开辟专门的二级域名，无店铺等级。买家在亚马逊上搜索产品并直接进入产品详情页面，不会记得卖家的店铺名称。卖家使用平台提供的统一的产品详情页面，可以节省大量时间和精力到物流配送和售后服务上。这种模式非常适合打造单品。

(3) Amazon listing hijack. This policy specifically refers to several different sellers who share the same product description page. For example, if seller A uploads product descriptions of a scooter, and seller B sells the same scooter, seller B does not need to create product descriptions, and can use the function of Amazon listing hijack. This policy is to provide customers with lower prices by helping them compare the prices from different sellers more conveniently. In order to ensure that there are more orders, sellers must not only guarantee low prices, but also make their best efforts on product quality and service.

飞轮跟卖政策。飞轮跟卖政策具体指几个不同的卖家如果销售一样的产品，就会共用一个产品详情页面。比如，A卖家已上传滑板车的产品信息，B卖家卖一模一样的滑板车，那么B卖家就不用自己上传产品详情，可以后台一键跟卖。该政策是为了给客户提供更低的价格，为了让消费者比价更方便。而卖家为了保证有更多的订单，不仅要保证低价，也要尽最大努力保证产品质量和服务。

## 2. Registration (店铺注册)

The accounts on Amazon are divided into self-registered accounts and sponsorship manager's global store accounts. You only need to contact Amazon's sponsorship manager to submit the materials and register according to the requirements of the sponsorship manager in order to get sponsorship manager's global store accounts. Here's the process for self-registered accounts.

亚马逊上的账户分为自注册账户和招商经理的全球开店账户两种。招商经理全球开店账户只需要联系亚马逊招商经理，提交材料，按照招商经理的要求注册即可。以下是自注册账户的流程。

Step 1: As shown in Figure 2-12, go to www. amazon. com and go to the bottom of the page. Click on "Sell On Amazon" and then click "Start Selling" to start the registration of Amazon North America site.

步骤一：如图 2-12 所示，进入 www.amazon.com 拉到页面底部，点击"Sell On Amazon"，进入以后点击"Start Selling"开始进行亚马逊北美站点的注册。

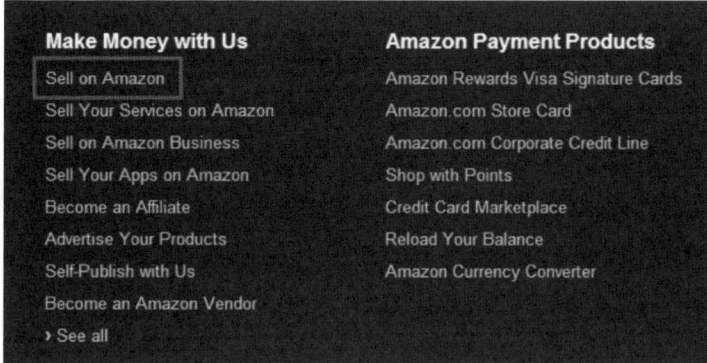

Figure 2-12（图2-12）

Step 2: As shown in Figure 2-13, fill in the name, email address, and login password as required. Amazon's account is unique, every business license, ID number, and IP can only register one account.

步骤二：如图 2-13 所示，根据要求填写姓名、邮箱地址，并且设置登录密码。亚马逊的账户具有唯一性，一个营业执照、一个身份证号码、一个 IP 只能注册一个账号。

Figure 2-13（图2-13）

Step 3: Fill in the legal name. If it is a business, enter the name of the business. If it is a person, enter the name of the person and agree to Amazon's terms, as shown in Figure 2-14.

步骤三：填写名称。如果是企业就输入企业的名称，如果是个人就输入个人的姓名，然后点击同意亚马逊的条款，如图2-14所示。

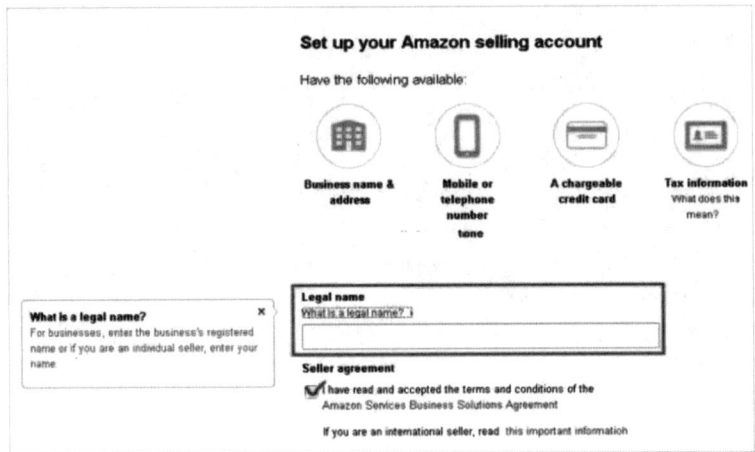

Figure 2-14（图2-14）

Step 4: As shown in Figure 2-15, fill in the English address, the unique official company name, and sales websites on other platforms. Finally, you need to get certification. There are usually three opportunities for certification. If you cannot always receive the phone, you can consider changing to receive a message. When you select the Call option, the page will pop up a page displaying the PIN and four digits. After the phone rings, you can enter them. When you select the SMS option, you will receive a four-digit PIN code and input it to the pop-up page. Note: After the verification is completed, you cannot return to this step to modify any information. Please check the contents of this page carefully before verifying.

步骤四：如图2-15所示，填写英文地址信息、唯一的公司显示名称以及其他平台销售网址。最后是认证，认证一般会有三次机会，如果一直接不到电话，可以考虑换成短信验证。选择电话验证时，页面会弹出一个页面显示PIN以及四位数字，电话响后，输入进去即可；选择短信验证时，您会收到一个四位的PIN编码，输入到弹出的页面即可。注意：验证完成后，无法退回至本步骤修改信息，请在验证前仔细检查本页内容。

**Hello. Tell us about your business**

Street address

City / Town　　　　　State / Region / Province
Beijing　　　　　　　Beijing

Country　　　　　　　ZIP / Postal Code
China　⇕　　　　　　102218

**Choose your unique business Display Name**
What is a business display name? ▸

**If you sell your products online, enter your website URL (optional)**
Why do we ask for this? ▸
www.example.com

Select an option to receive a PIN to verify your phone number
◉ Call　○ SMS
Telephone number
█ ▾ -
E.g. +1 206 266 1000

Phone Verification Language

Figure 2-15（图2-15）

Step 5: Bind the credit card. As shown in Figure 2-16, fill in the credit card information as required by Amazon, including credit card number, expiration date, cardholder name, billing address, and set your payment method. Note: Please confirm that the default address is the same as the credit card billing address. If it is different, please fill in the address in English or Pinyin. The credit card holder and the account registrant do not need to be the same person, and the company account can also use a personal credit card.

步骤五:绑定信用卡。如图2-16所示,按照亚马逊的要求填写信用卡信息,包括信用卡卡号、有效期、持卡人姓名、账单地址,并设置收款方式。注意:请确认默认地址信息是否与信用卡账单地址相同。如不同,请使用英文或者拼音填写地址。信用卡持卡人与账户注册人无须为同一人,公司账户也可使用个人信用卡。

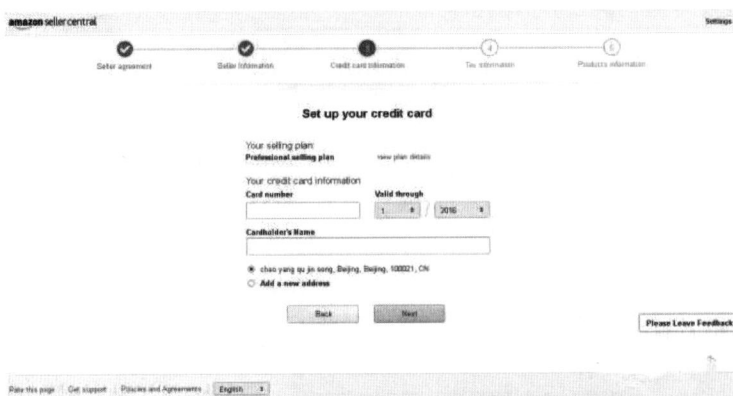

Figure 2-16（图2-16）

Step 6: Start tax authentication. If you are not a US person, select No, and other tax information should be filled out as required, as shown in Figure 2-17. Note: If your account is a company, please confirm your company's mailing address; if your account is a person, after confirming your mailing address, please make sure that you don't conform to any of the options.

步骤六:开始税务身份验证。如果非美国人员,就选No,其他税务信息按要求如实填写即可,如图2-17所示。注意:如果您的账户是公司,请确认您公司的邮寄地址;如果您的账户是个人,在确认邮寄地址后,请确认您不符合其中的任何一项。

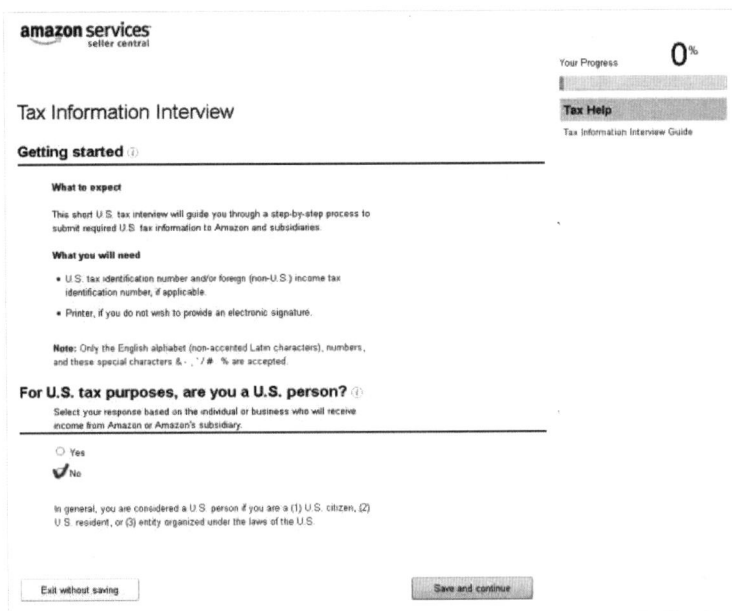

Figure 2-17（图2-17）

Step 7: As shown in Figure 2-18, preview the content on W-8BEN and agree to provide an electronic signature. Finally, click "Submit" and the system will generate a W-8 form.

步骤七：如图 2-18 所示，预览 W-8BEN 内容并同意提供电子签名，最后点击提交，系统会生成 W-8 表格。

Figure 2-18（图 2-18）

Step 8: Fill in the product information and select the sales category. As shown in Figure 2-19, Amazon will give you some questions to answer, in order to understand the nature and the number of the products you plan to start selling. Based on this information, Amazon will recommend relevant tools and information for your account. After the seller's identity verification and the above steps are completed, you can log in to the Amazon Seller Central for sales.

步骤八:填写产品信息,选择销售分类。如图2-19所示,亚马逊会列举一些问题请您回答,借此了解您的产品性质和开始销售时计划的数量。基于这些信息,亚马逊会推荐适合您账户的相关工具和信息。之后再进行卖家身份验证,以上步骤都完成后你就可以登录亚马逊后台进行销售了。

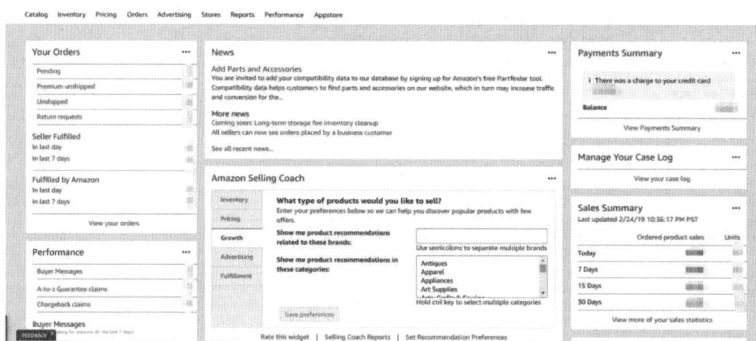

Figure 2-19 (图2-19)

## 3. Analysis of Amazon Seller Central (亚马逊平台操作解析)

Amazon Seller Central is the beginning of sellers' sales. Sellers can enter the account number and password to log in to Amazon Seller Central. The page after login is shown in Figure 2-20. The interface language can be switched at the top of the page. Available languages are English, Chinese, German, Spanish, French, Italian, Japanese, and Korean.

卖家中心是卖家开展销售的起点,卖家可以输入账号和密码登录到卖家账号后台主页,登录后的页面如图2-20所示。在页面上方可切换界面语言,可选语言包括英语、中文、德语、西班牙语、法语、意大利语、日语和韩语。

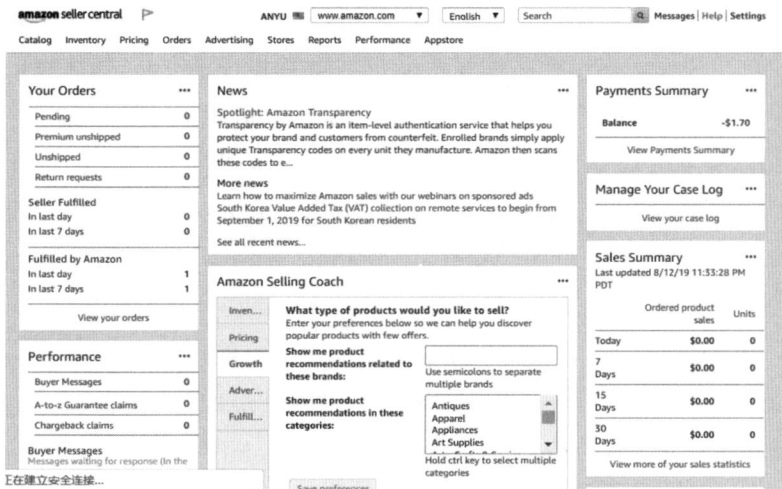

Figure 2-20（图2-20）

Click Settings in the top right corner, you can see Logout, Account Info, Notification Preferences, Login Settings, Return Settings, Gift Options, Shipping Settings, Tax Settings, User Permissions, Your Info & Policies, and Fulfillment by Amazon. Account Info mainly includes holiday settings, seller information, payment information, business information and so on. If the seller chooses the self-delivery mode, remember to open holiday setting because domestic logistics will take a break during National Holiday and Spring Festival, so the store will stop selling. FBA (Fulfillment by Amazon) shipments are not affected and there is no need to turn on holiday setting.

点击右上角的账户后台设置,可以看到注销、账户信息、通知偏好、登录设置、退货设置、礼品服务、运费设置、税务设置、用户设置、卖家信息及政策和亚马逊物流选项。在账户信息设置中,主要包含假期设置、卖家资料、付款信息、业务信息等。如果卖家选择的是"自发货"模式,由于国庆和春节期间国内物流休息,卖家需开启假期设置,这样店铺就停止销售了。亚马逊物流服务则不受影响,不需要开启假期设置。

You can create a product by clicking "Add New Item" or "Batch Upload Items" under "Inventory", where the "Add New Item" option has exactly the same function with "Add Item under Catalog". Creating products includes listing hijack and self-built products. It should be noted that the products with pictures on the product description page are brand registered products and other sellers cannot use the function of Amazon listing hijack. Moreover, if the product has a brand, you must display the brand at the beginning of the title. In addition, there are functions of inventory reports, global sales, management inventory and the like.

点击库存下的添加新商品或批量上传商品可以创建产品,其中的添加新商品选项和目录下的添加商品功能一模一样。创建产品包括跟卖和自建产品,要注意的是产品详情页有图片的即为品牌备案的产品,不能跟卖。并且如果商品有品牌,一定要在标题最前面显示品牌。此外,亚马逊还有库存报告、全球销售、管理库存等功能。

The Pricing option allows you to query and manage product pricing, such as viewing pricing dashboards and managing pricing. The orders option mainly shows the process of orders, including viewing order details, downloading order reports, and viewing return orders. Advertising is a promotion that sellers make on Amazon, such as discounts, price reductions and so on. Sellers can set up all in-site advertising campaigns here. Among them, "Seckill" is one of the most commonly used promotion activities for sellers to advertise inside the station. If the system recommends the products in the store, the seller can report it by himself and participate in promotion activities on Prime Day, Halloween, and Christmas, etc.

定价选项可以查询和管理产品定价,如查看定价仪表板、管理定价。订单选项主要是订单的处理,包括查看订单详情、下载订单报告、查看订单退货情况。广告是卖家在亚马逊上做的促销活动,如打折、降价活动等。卖家可以在这里设置所有的站内广告活动。其中"秒杀"是卖家做站内推广时最常用的一个功能,如果系统推荐了店铺内的产品,卖家可以自主提报,参加如会员促销日、万圣节促销和圣诞节促销等活动。

Reports and Performance are Amazon's data support modes. Reports page includes four major types of reports: Inventory Reports, Order Reports, Business Reports, and Advertising Reports. In the Performance column, sellers can view Customer Satisfaction, Feedback, A-to-Z Guarantee Claims, Chargeback Claims and Performance Notification. Customer Satisfaction includes order defect rate, merchandise policy compliance and delivery performance. Feedback is the customer's evaluation of store logistics and delivery timeliness. These two items are related to the security of seller account. It will be better to check it every day.

报告和绩效属于亚马逊的数据支持模块。报告页面下又包括库存报告、订单报告、业务报告及广告报告四大类型的报告内容。在绩效栏,卖家可以查看账户状况、反馈、亚马逊商城交易保障索赔、信用卡拒付索赔和业绩通知。账户状况包括订单缺陷率、商品政策合规性和配送绩效,反馈是客户对于店铺物流和配送时效的评价,这两项都关系到卖家账号安全,最好每天查看一下。

## Section Three / **Wish**

### 1. Characteristics of Wish（Wish平台的特点）

Founded in 2011 in Silicon Valley, San Francisco, Wish is the largest mobile e-commerce shopping platform in North America, with 95% of orders coming from the mobile terminal. The platform will recommend the products to customers who may be interested in them through an accurate algorithm system to attract potential consumers. The mobile page of Wish is shown in Figure 2-21.

Wish于2011年成立于美国旧金山硅谷，是北美最大的移动电商购物平台，95%的订单来自移动端。平台会通过精确的算法系统，将顾客可能感兴趣的商品信息推送给他们，吸引潜在消费者。Wish的移动端页面如图2-21所示。

Figure 2-21（图2-21）

In 2014, Wish established a wholly owned subsidiary in China with an annual operating income of more than 400 million dollars. In 2015, there were nearly 200 million users who shop on Wish. In 2016, the overseas warehouse was launched, and the policy of the sellers who opened the overseas warehouses was tilted. As of early May 2017, Wish Mobile App was ranked number one among all shopping Apps in 27 countries around the world. In 2018, Wish had supplied more than 200 million products to more than 350 million consumers worldwide, with more than 90 million monthly active users, 125,000 active merchants, and a daily order peak of 2 million. The orders were mainly from the United States, Canada, Europe and other parts of the world.

2014年,Wish在中国成立全资子公司,年经营收益超过4亿美元。2015年,移动端用户已将近2亿用户。2016年推出海外仓,并对开通海外仓的卖家做出政策上的倾斜。截至2017年5月初,Wish手机App在全球27个国家的购物类App中排名第一。2018年,Wish累计向全球超过3.5亿的消费者供应了逾2亿款商品,月活跃用户超过9000万,活跃商户达12.5万,日出货量峰值达到200万单,订单主要来自美国、加拿大、欧洲等国家和地区。

Wish platform is mainly for developed regions in Europe and America, but the sellers are almost from China. Even among the international sellers, there are many products that are made in China. Wish recommending style is that customers first see picture, then price, most of the orders are impulse shopping. Although the platform is dedicated to low prices, sales through price wars are not sustainable for the platform. If you rely on free shipping with order over 3 dollars, 30-day arrival business model to sell low-quality products and maintain profits, buyers will not patronize or recommend your store to friends. For long-term operation, sellers must improve product quality and service to create a brand with high quality.

Wish平台主要面向欧美发达地区,但是卖家几乎来自中国,即使在国际卖家中也有很多在销售中国制造的产品。Wish推送的风格是让客户先看到图片,然后才是价格,大多属于"冲动性"购物。虽然该平台致力于低价,但在平台上通过价格战销售是不可持续的。如果依靠3美元包邮、30天到货的经营模式来销售低质量的产品,维持利润,买家是不会再次光顾或推荐给朋友的。为了长久地经营,卖家要提高产品质量和服务,打造优质品牌。

There are many core elements for Wish to recommend products, including violation rate, late rate, cancellation rate, delivery rate, return rate, recommendation conversion rate, etc. The better these indicators, the more the system will help you to promote. However, if the recommendation conversion rate of the product is not up to standard, the system will transfer the recommendation opportunity to other products that meet the conditions. Therefore, it is important to research, develop popular products and optimize products.

Wish推送产品的核心要素众多,包括违规率、迟发率、取消率、签收率、退货率、推送转化率等,这些指标越好,系统就会越多地帮你推送。但如果推送的商品推送转化率不达标,那么系统就会把推送的机会转给下一个符合该条件的商品。因此,调研、开发受欢迎的商品并优化商品至关重要。

(1) **Advantages of Wish (平台优势)**

Wish is committed to providing consumers with a simple and fun shopping software. Compared with other platforms, shopping on Wish is more entertaining, making the boring online shopping experience easier, and even making shopping a pleasant experience. Thousands of designs and unique algorithms can accurately locate thousands of consumers and help sellers accurately recommend products to customers. Moreover, Wish platform is very simple to operate, and the publishing process is simple with all Chinese language background. There is no need to make multiple shipping templates, no online customer service, and the operating cost is very low.

Wish致力于为消费者提供一款简便、有趣的购物软件。和其他平台相比,在Wish上购物娱乐性更强,可以让沉闷乏味的闲逛变得更加简单,甚至让购物变成了一种乐趣。千人千面的设计和独有的算法可以精准定位成千上万的消费者,帮助卖家将产品精准地推送给消费者。并且,Wish平台操作非常简单,发布流程简便,全中文后台,无须制定多重运费模板,不需要在线客服,运营成本非常低。

(2) **Marketable Products (适销产品)**

At present, the main categories of Wish include fashion apparel, 3C accessories, ornaments, hobbies, mother and baby items, and home improvements, etc. Wish users are mainly middle-aged and young people between the ages of 15 and 40. Most of them are female users, and young users account for about half of Wish users. The consumption of young groups has more obvious "impulsiveness" and "fashion preference", and the trend-oriented products are obviously more in line with their tastes. Moreover, since Wish is mostly for mobile shopping, it is also important to achieve maximum exposure of the product during fragmented browsing time. Based on the above platform features, all kinds of new and unique products, fashion and topical products are more suitable for sale on Wish.

目前 Wish 平台主要销售的类目包括时尚服饰、3C 配件、配饰、兴趣爱好、母婴、家居等。Wish 的用户主要集中在 15 至 40 岁的中青年群体,以女性用户居多,青年用户占 Wish 用户的一半左右。年轻群体的消费具有较为明显的冲动性和时尚偏好,潮流趋势性的产品显然更符合他们的口味。而且,由于 Wish 属于移动端购物,如何在碎片化的浏览时间里实现产品的最大曝光也至关重要。基于以上平台特征,各类新颖奇特的产品、时尚类产品更适合在 Wish 平台上销售。

## 2. Registration (店铺注册)

Step 1: As shown in Figure 2-22, log in to china-merchant.wish.com and click "Open the Store Immediately".

步骤一:如图 2-22 所示,登录 china-merchant.wish.com 并点击"立即开店"。

Figure 2-22 (图 2-22)

Step 2: Fill in the username and other information at the page of "Start to Create Your Wish Store". Enter the phone number to receive the verification code and click "Create Store", as shown in Figure 2-23.

步骤二:在"开始创建您的 Wish 店铺"页面填写用户名等信息。输入手机号码用于接收验证码,点击"创建店铺",如图 2-23 所示。

Figure 2-23（图2-23）

Step 3: Read the merchant agreement and click on the bottom box after reading all the information, as shown in Figure 2-24.

步骤三：阅读商户协议，并在全部阅读完后点击最下方的选框，如图2-24所示。

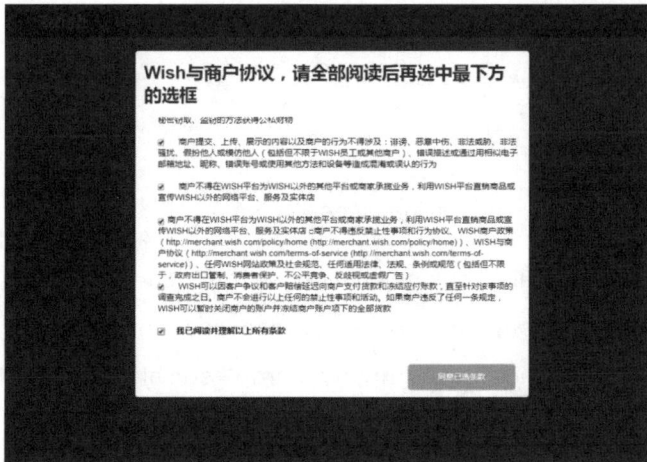

Figure 2-24（图2-24）

Step 4: Check the email, enter the email inbox, and click to confirm the email or the URL will jump directly to the merchant background.

步骤四：查收邮件，进入邮箱点击确认邮箱或者 URL 后会直接跳转到商户后台。

Step 5: As shown in Figure 2-25, fill in the account information. In the process of filling information, you need to pay attention to the following points: ①The account name is in English, but do not contain the word "Wish" or well-known brand words. If the store involves infringement, it will affect the time of the review. Once the store name is determined, it cannot be changed. ② It is suggested to use Chinese Pinyin of the real name as the last name and first name.

步骤五：如图 2-25 所示，填写账号信息。填写的过程中，需要注意以下几点：①账号名称用英文，但是不要使用含有"Wish"的字样或知名品牌词，如果店铺名称涉及侵权，则会影响审核的时间。店铺名称一旦确定将无法更改；②姓氏和名字建议使用真实姓名的汉语拼音。

店铺名称（英文）　　　　　　　　　　　　取名建议 ?

不能包含"Wish"字样

您的真实姓名（中文）　　　　　　　　一旦提交将无法修改 ?

姓氏　　　　　　　　　　　名字

办公地址

中国大陆　　　　　　　　　　　　　　　　⬍

安徽省　　　　　⬍　　　安庆市　　　　　⬍

街道地址

邮编

邮编

Figure 2-25（图 2-25）

Step 6: Please prepare business license, ID card of the juridical person, company receipt information, etc., for enterprise account authentication. As shown in Figure 2-26, please fill in the company name, social credit code, name and ID card number of the juridical person as required, and upload a clear color photo of the business license. Note: privately-owned business cannot be used as corporate accounts.

步骤六：企业账号认证，请准备好企业营业执照、法人代表身份证和公司收款信息等。

如图 2-26 所示,请根据要求填写企业的公司名称、统一社会信用代码、法人代表姓名和身份证号码等信息,上传清晰的营业执照彩色照片。注意:个体工商户不可作为企业账户。

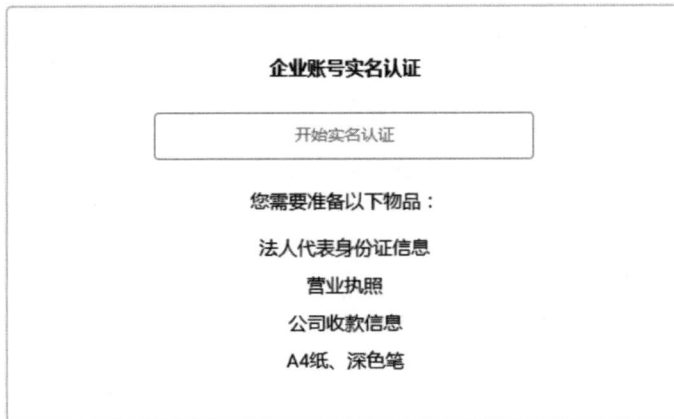

Figure 2-26 (图 2-26)

Step 7: Please prepare a camera, an identity card of the juridical person, a dark pen and an A4 white paper. Note: ①) Use a digital camera or a mobile phone with more than 5 million pixels (do not use the beauty function); ② Photo resolution and file size (within 3MB) will affect your real-name authentication. Please choose the photo tool carefully; ③ The entire authentication process needs to be completed within 15 minutes. As shown in Figure 2-27.

步骤七:请准备好拍照工具、法人代表身份证、深色笔及一张 A4 白纸。注意:①使用数码相机或拍照像素 500 万以上的手机(不要使用美颜功能的机型);②照片清晰度和文件大小(3MB 以内)将影响您的实名认证,请谨慎选择拍照工具;③整个认证必须在 15 分钟内完成。如图 2-27 所示。

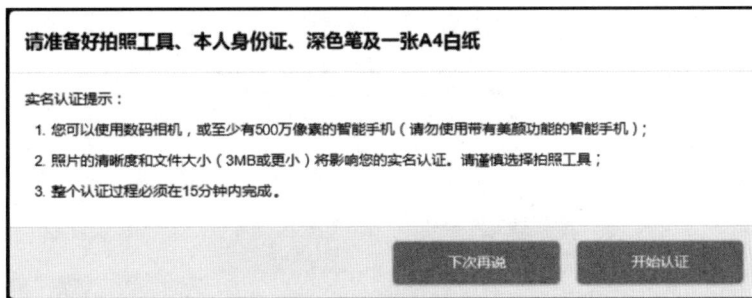

Figure 2-27 (图 2-27)

Step 8: Enter the payment option. Here the platform will show you how to add payment information so that you can receive payment after the business is completed on the platform, as shown in Figure 2-28.

步骤八:进入支付选择。此处平台会展示如何添加收款信息,以便Wish业务开展后能正常收到货款。如图2-28所示。

Figure 2-28 (图2-28)

Note: from 0:00 (World Standard Time) on October 1, 2018, all newly registered stores must pay a pre-paid registration fee of 2,000 dollars, as shown in Figure 2-29.

注意:自2018年10月1日0时(世界标准时间)起,新注册的店铺须缴纳2000美元的店铺预缴注册费。如图2-29所示。

Figure 2-29 (图2-29)

After the payment is completed, the page will display "Complete Payment", indicating that you have successfully paid the store pre-paid registration fee. Go back to the business backend homepage and see if we are reviewing your store, it indicates that the registration process has been completed.

完成支付后,页面会显示"支付成功",说明您已成功缴纳店铺预缴注册费。返回商户后台首页后,如果看到我们正在审核您的店铺,则表示注册流程已全部完成。

## 3. Wish Platform Analysis (Wish平台解析)

As shown in Figure 2-30, Wish merchant platform includes information on products, orders, merchant issues, and performance, etc. The following are some of the issues that need to be addressed during operation.

如图2-30所示,Wish商户平台包括产品、订单、商户问题、业绩等信息。以下是在平台操作过程中,需要注意的几项问题。

Figure 2-30 (图2-30)

(1) During the Spring Festival, due to the impact of domestic suppliers and logistics, sellers generally need to open the holiday mode. Under this mode, all products of the store will be removed, and no new orders will be generated during the holiday mode. We can click on setting on the homepage to find the holiday mode. Click to start holiday mode, as shown in Figure 2-31. If there are both direct delivery products and Wish Express products in the store, the seller can open special edition holiday mode of Wish Express.

(1)春节期间,由于国内供应商和物流受到影响,卖家一般需要开启假期模式,店铺的所有产品都将被下架,假期模式期间将不会产生新的订单。我们可以点击首页账户设置,找到假期模式,点击打开即可开启假期模式,如图2-31所示。如果店铺里既有直发类产品也有Wish Express类产品,那么卖家可以开启Wish Express专项版的假期模式。

Figure 2-31 (图2-31)

(2) The pricing of products affects the exposure and order quantity of products. Product pricing can be calculated by market research or profit formula. Wish does not charge platform fee but charge a commission of 15% of each transaction. Products can generally be priced using the following formula: Product Price = (Cost + Packaging Cost + International Shipping) / US Dollar Exchange Rate / (1−15%) / (1−Profit %). Sellers can also set different profit margins based on analyzing the competitor's product information, international market, and life cycle of the product to maximize the total profit. At the same time, the freight should not be set too high. For example, if the same product is sold for 6 dollars, it will be more acceptable to set the price at $5+$1 than $4+$2 for customers.

(2)产品的定价影响产品的曝光率和订单量,产品定价可以通过市场调研法或利润公式计算而来。Wish平台不收取平台费用,而是按照每笔成交金额的15%收取佣金。产品一般可以用以下公式进行定价:产品定价=(成本+包装耗材+国际运费) / 美元汇率 / (1−15%) / (1−利润%)。卖家也可以根据该产品的竞争对手情况、市场情况、产品所处的生命周期等设置不同的利润率,以获得总利润最大化。同时,运费也不宜设置过高,比如同样是卖6美元的产品,价格设置成5+1美元比4+2美元更容易让客户接受。

(3) Wish puts a lot of efforts into fighting against counterfeit products. Sellers cannot use the following pictures if the background has famous brand identification, the label is intentionally blurred, the model face is blurred or tailored, or there is

design infringement. Therefore, sellers need to publish original content and images to sell their own brands or licensed branded products. Sellers can view products that are judged to be counterfeit in the sellers' background. The counterfeit product rate refers to the number of items that are judged to be counterfeit over a certain period of time. If the counterfeit product rate of a store reaches higher than 0.5%, it will lose the qualification of an honest store.

（3）Wish对仿品的打击力度非常大,背景有名牌商品标识、标签故意模糊、模特脸模糊或剪裁及外观设计侵权等图片都不能用。因此,卖家需要发布原创的内容和图片,售卖自创品牌或得到授权的品牌产品。卖家可以在Wish后台查看被判定为伪造品的产品。仿品率指的是在一段时期内,被判定为仿品的数量除以经过审核的商品总量,仿品率高于0.5%的店铺会失去诚信店铺的资格。

(4) Honest stores on Wish have many advantages, including getting more traffic support and the products will appear faster in search results. Therefore, in addition to counterfeit product rate, sellers also need to pay attention to data in sellers' center such as effective tracking rate, delayed delivery rate, 30-day average rating and refund rate. These indicators are indispensable in the process of evaluating honest stores. Sellers need to continue to pay attention to the indicators which have not yet reached the requirement of an honest store, and then make plans to optimize the operation process. For example, the warning line of refund rate is 10%. If a product refund rate is higher than 10% for a long time, Wish will warn the store. After the warning, the refund rate cannot be reduced, then Wish will put this product directly off the shelf. Therefore, sellers need to notice abnormal products in time and make corresponding improvements.

（4）Wish平台上的诚信店铺有众多优势,包括获得更多的流量支持、让产品更快出现在搜索结果中等。因此,除了仿品率,卖家还需要关注有效跟踪率、延迟发货率、30天平均评分和退款率等后台数据。这些指标在考核诚信店铺的过程中缺一不可。卖家需要持续关注哪些指标尚未达到诚信店铺,有针对性地进行运营优化。比如,退款率的警告线是10%。如果一款产品退款率长期高于10%,Wish会对店铺发出警告,警告之后,如果退款率还不能下降,那么Wish会把这款产品直接下架。因此,卖家需要及时发现产品异常,并做出相应改善。

# Section Four / **eBay**

## 易 贝

## 1. Characteristics of eBay (易贝平台的特点)

Founded in September 1995 by Pierre Omidyar under the name Auctionweb in California, eBay Group is a global leader in the field of business and payment, providing opportunities for companies of all sizes to compete and develop together. eBay is the world's largest online trading market. With its online trading sites and rigorous credit evaluation systems in many countries around the world, eBay can help SMEs realize their dream of cross-border c-commerce. The official website is shown in Figure 2-32.

易贝集团于1995年9月由皮埃尔·奥米迪亚以Auctionweb的名称创立于美国加利福尼亚州,是全球商务和支付行业的领跑者,为不同规模的商家提供公平竞争、共同发展的机会。易贝是全球最大的网上交易市场,凭借遍布全球多个国家的网上贸易站点和严谨的信用评价系统,可以帮助中小企业实现跨境电商创业梦想。官网如图2-32所示。

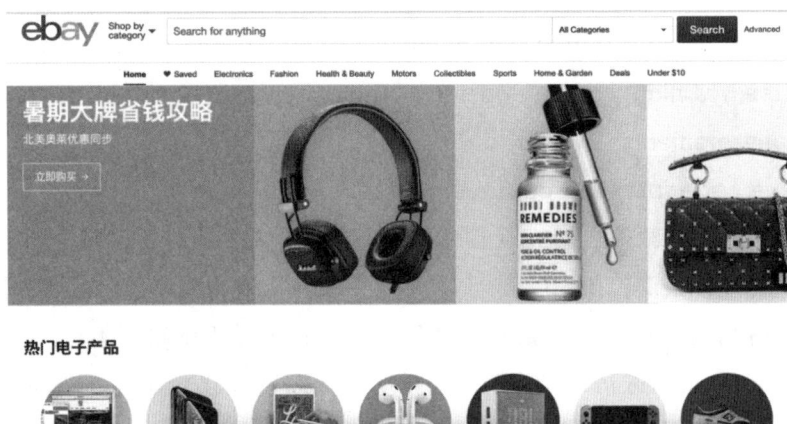

Figure 2-32 (图2-32)

eBay entered China in 2002 through the acquisition of China's C2C platform Eachnet, using a global strategy to operate the Chinese business and focusing on auction, while Chinese consumers are more inclined to fixed prices. The localization of Taobao won the trust of more Chinese sellers. Moreover, at that time Taobao did not charge sellers while eBay China charges sellers when they publish a product. In 2012, eBay announced its withdrawal from the Chinese market due to a severe decline in market share. But at present, eBay has opened up Chinese B2C cross-border e-commerce market and has become an indispensable platform for cross-border e-commerce sellers.

易贝于2002年通过收购中国的C2C平台易趣进驻中国,用全球战略经营中国业务,专注拍卖业务,而中国消费者更倾向于固定价格。淘宝的本土化赢得了更多中国卖家的信任,并且其在当时还不对卖家收取佣金,而易贝中国站需要收取上架费。2012年,易贝由于市场份额严重下降,宣布退出中国市场。但目前,易贝已开辟了中国B2C跨境电商市场,成为跨境电商卖家不可或缺的平台。

As one of the world's largest online trading platforms, eBay enables everyone around the world to realize the desire to purchase at anytime and anywhere. On eBay, millions of items are published every day. The commodity types are all-encompassing, such as commemorative cards, antiques, dolls and other collectibles, and commodities like used cars, books, clothes and electronics can be traded on it. Transactions on eBay are all over the world and eBay has sites in 26 countries and regions, including the United States, Britain, Australia, Canada, France, Germany and so on. eBay has 179 million active buyers and 27 million global sellers in 190 countries and regions. On December 20, 2018, the 2018 World Top 500 brands list was released, and eBay ranked 47th.

作为全球最大的在线交易平台之一,易贝让世界各地的每一个人实现了随时随地购买其所需物品的愿望。在易贝上,每天有数以百万计的商品被刊登,商品种类包罗万象,如纪念卡、古董、玩偶之类的收藏品,二手车、书籍、服装、电子产品等商品都可以在上面进行交易。易贝的交易遍布全球各地,并在多个国家和地区设有站点,包括美国、英国、澳大利亚、加拿大、法国、德国等26个国家和地区。易贝拥有1.79亿活跃买家和2700万全球卖家,覆盖190个国家和地区。2018年12月20日,2018世界品牌500强排行榜发布,易贝名列47位。

Compared with other platforms, eBay aims mainly at mature markets. So the entry threshold is higher, and the requirements for sellers, products, services and logistics quality are relatively stricter. The rules on eBay tend to protect buyers more. Therefore, if seller wants to get the popularity from buyer on eBay, it's not enough to have good commodities. Other aspects like localization services including overseas warehouses, local brand and packaging should be excellent. And the price should also be ensured to be competitive enough.

　　与其他平台相比，由于易贝主要面向的是成熟市场，因此准入门槛较高，对卖家、商品、服务、物流质量等方面的要求也相对更严格，易贝平台内的规则也更偏向于买家。所以，卖家如果想在易贝平台得到买家的青睐，只有商品好是不够的，其他方面的实力也要过硬才行，如本地化服务，包括海外仓、本地品牌、包装等，还要保证价格具有足够的竞争力。

　　(1) Modes of Sale (易贝的销售方式)

eBay offers sellers three ways to place their products.

　　易贝为卖家提供了3种展示商品的方式。

Auction method. As shown in Figure 2-33, auction refers to sell through price bidding. The highest price wins. This is the common method for eBay sellers. The seller sets the starting price and totally time for auction. The buyer with the highest bid before the product goes offline can get the product with the winning bid price. The seller needs to pay a certain percentage of the publishing fee according to the starting price set by himself and the transaction fee according to the final price.

　　拍卖方式。如图2-33所示，拍卖指通过竞拍的方式进行销售，价高者得，这是易贝卖家常用的销售方式。卖家设置商品的起拍价格和在线时间，商品下线前出价最高的买家即可用中标价格获得商品。卖家需要根据自己设定的起拍价缴纳一定比例的刊登费。此外，根据物品最后的成交价格，卖家还需缴纳一定比率的成交费。

Figure 2-33 (图2-33)

Fixed price method. As shown in Figure 2-34, the fixed price method is to sell by fixed price. Buyers can purchase directly with the listed price. If the seller opens the bargain function (Best Offer), buyers can also bargain with the seller to buy the product.

　　一口价方式。如图2-34所示，一口价方式就是以定价的方式来展示物品。买家可以用定价直接购得商品,如果卖家开启了议价功能,买家也可以跟卖家讨价还价来购得商品。

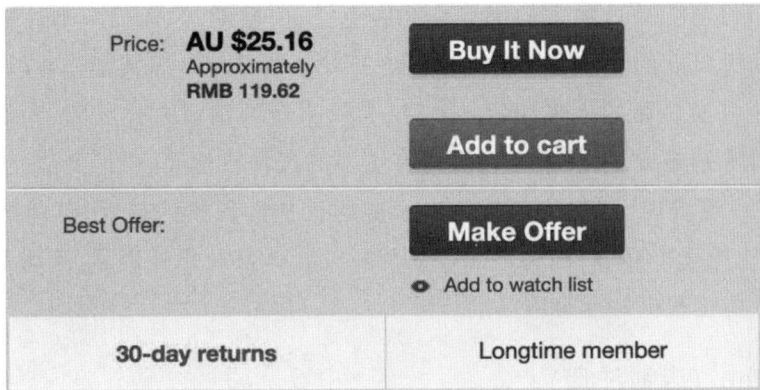

Figure 2-34 (图 2-34)

Auction + fixed price method. The seller chooses the aution method when selling, he sets the minimum starting price, and also sets a satisfactory reserve price according to his own judgement on the value of the item, which is called fixed price. This auction + fixed price method can integrate all the advantages of the auction method and the fixed price method, allowing buyers to flexibly choose the purchase method according to their own needs and circumstances. It also brings more business opportunities to the seller.

拍卖+一口价综合方式。卖家在销售商品时选择拍卖方式,设置最低起拍价的同时,再根据自己对物品价值的评判设置一个满意的保底价,也就是一口价。这种拍卖+一口价的方式能够同时综合拍卖方式和一口价方式的所有优势,能让买家根据自身需要和情况灵活地选择购买方式,也能为卖家带来更多的商机。

(2) Advantages of eBay (易贝平台的优势)

Compared with other platform, eBay's biggest advantage is free shop opening and low threshold. You can easily start foreign trade sales at eBay's global sites only by simply registering an eBay account. The shop operation is relatively simple and the investment is not much. It's suitable for people with certain foreign trade resources to operate. Moreover, eBay has flexible sales modes and provides sellers with sales methods including auctions and fixed price method, which provides sellers and buyers more choices. Although opening the store is free, publishing products will charge a fee. At the beginning, reputation should be accumulated through the auction. The cycle for new orders is relatively long. Electronic products, fashion products, auto parts product, sports & outdoor products, home and gardening products on eBay are all hot items. But they are also different according to sites.

与其他平台相比,易贝最大的优势是开店免费、门槛低,只需简单地注册一个易贝账户,就可以在易贝设立的全球各个站点轻松地开展外贸销售。店铺操作比较简单,投入不大,适合有一定外贸资源的人来经营。并且,易贝平台的销售方式灵活,为卖家提供了包括拍卖、一口价等销售方式,让卖家和买家有更多的选择。然而,虽然开店是免费的,但上架产品会收取一定费用。此外,刚开始卖家要通过拍卖积累信誉,出订单的周期相对较长。易贝平台上电子产品、时尚类产品、汽配类产品、体育及户外用品、家居及园艺产品都属于热销品类,但也根据站点有所区别。

## 2. Registration (店铺注册)

Step 1: Chinese sellers can register on eBay Hong Kong and input the following address: https://www.ebay.com.hk/ to be registered as an eBay member. Click it to create an account to enter account registration page or log in with Facebook or Google. As shown in Figure 2-35.

步骤一:中国卖家可以在易贝香港进行注册,输入如下链接地址https://www.ebay.com. hk/,登记成为易贝会员。单击建立账户,进入账号注册页面,也可以用脸书或谷歌账号登录。如图2-35所示。

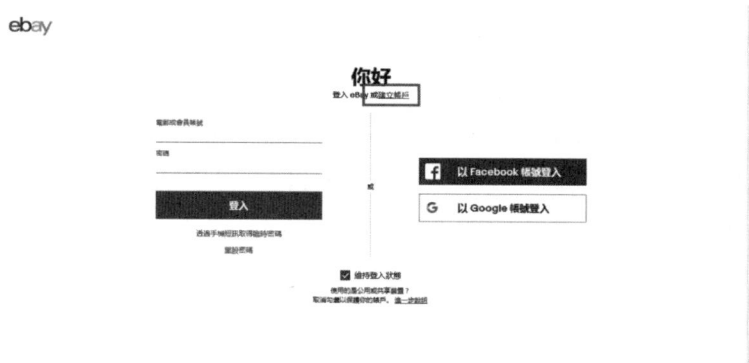

Figure 2-35 (图2-35)

Step 2: Input personal information on the registration page as shown in Figure 2-36. The entered email must be real and valid. Subsequently, log in to eBay account with this email.

步骤二:如图2-36所示,在注册页面输入个人信息。输入的电子邮箱地址必须真实有效,后续登录易贝账户使用需该邮箱登录。

Figure 2-36 (图 2-36)

Step 3: As shown in Figure 2-37, click "Register" to become a member and enter the seller authentication page. Fill in your personal contact information and click "Continue" to enter the phone number confirmation page. Enter the security code received by the phone in the "Security Code" input box, and then click "Continue" to complete the registration. Then the process of personal eBay account registration and authentication is completed.

步骤三:如图 2-37 所示,单击登记成为会员,进入卖家认证页面,输入完个人联络资料后单击继续,进入电话号码确认页面。在"验证码"输入框中输入手机收到的验证码,随后单击继续按钮完成账号注册。个人易贝账号注册认证完成。

Figure 2-37 (图 2-37)

Step 4: Modify the account name. When registering an eBay account, the system generates a personal account by default. Since the account is a random alphanumeric combination and the irregular account name is easily banned, it is recommended to modify it to a meaningful English word combination. The specific modification method is as follows: Re-log in the account, as shown in Figure 2-38. Click the personal account name. Select the account setting button in the pop-up window and enter "My Account" page.

步骤四:修改账号名称。注册易贝账号时,系统会默认生成一个个人账号,由于该账号是随机字母数字的组合,无规则的账户名容易被封号,因此建议修改为有意义的英文单词组合。具体修改方法如下:重新登录账号,单击个人账户资料,在弹出的窗口中选择账户设定,进入"我的账户"页面。(如图2-38所示)

Figure 2-38 (图2-38)

As shown in Figure 2-39, click "Account" to enter the personal account information page. Click "Edit" which is after the member account in the profile and enter the member account modification page. Fill in the new member account name according to the requirements. Note: After the personal ID is modified, it cannot be modified again within 30 days. Please be careful when modify it.

如图2-39所示,单击账户,进入个人账户资料页面,然后单击个人资料中的会员账号后的"编辑",进入会员账号修改页面,根据提示输入新的会员账号即可。注意:个人账号ID修改后,30天内无法再次修改,请谨慎修改。

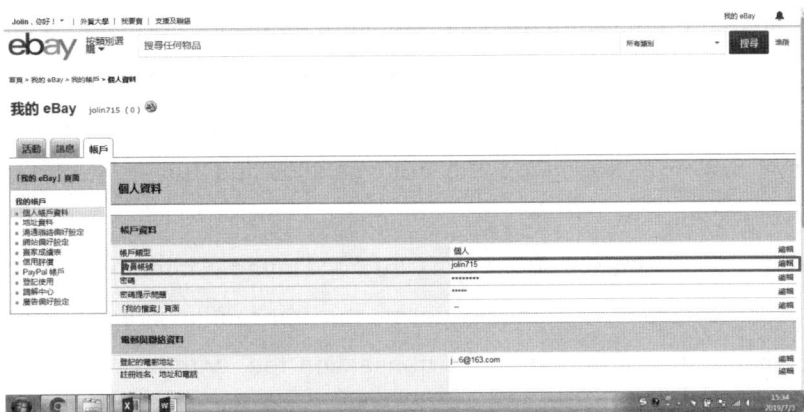

Figure 2-39 (图 2-39)

## 3. eBay Analysis（易贝平台解析）

Since July 2018, eBay had announced the termination of its partnership with long-term payment partner PayPal and announced a new partnership with its rivals, Apple and Square. As a simple, secure and private payment, Apple Pay will be one of the first payment offered in eBay's new payment solution. eBay will stop using PayPal as its back-end payment service in 2020, but before that time sellers can still collect money by signing up for a PayPal account.

自 2018 年 7 月，易贝宣布终止与长期支付伙伴 PayPal 的合作，宣布与后者的竞争对手苹果和 Square 达成新的伙伴关系。Apple Pay 作为一种简单、有保障且私密的付款方式，将成为易贝全新支付方案中提供的首批付款方式之一。易贝将于 2020 年停止使用 PayPal 作为其后端支付服务，但是在这之前，卖家仍可以通过注册绑定 PayPal 账户进行收款。

To open a store on eBay, you must know eBay's charging standards in order to properly price the product and obtain the target profit. The fees that seller needs to pay include the basic fee and the optional fee. The basic fee includes the publication fee, transaction fee and PayPal fee. Optional fees mainly refer to the fees of store subscription and featured function.

在易贝上开店，一定要了解易贝的收费标准，才能对产品进行合理定价，获得目标利润。卖家需要支付的费用包括基本费用和可选费用两大部分。基本费用包含刊登费、成交费及 PayPal 费用。可选费用主要指订阅店铺、特色功能费。

The publication fee refers to the fee that the seller has to pay for listing. But according to the seller type, a certain free quota can be obtained each month. A publication fee of 0.3 dollars will be charged when the number of publications exceeds the free amount. For the free part, some categories or certain products are not included in the free amount. The transaction fee refers to the fee charged when the seller successfully sells the product. The transaction fee, including product and logistics costs, which is based on the cost paid by the buyer. Without opening a store, the transaction fee for most products is 10% of the total sales. But the maximum is no more than 750 dollars. In the United States site, if the seller's account sales drop to below standard seller, the transaction fee rate will increase a certain percentage. PayPal fee includes transaction fee, withdrawal fee and currency exchange fee. According to the monthly collection amount and the payment method, it has different rates. The fee of store subscription is the monthly fee charged for the seller who opens the store on eBay. The charge is based on the site and store level. The fee of featured function means the extra fee of adding some special features to the item. It is decided by the seller on whether to select this function or not.

刊登费指卖家刊登产品需要缴纳的费用,不过根据卖家类型每个月可以获得一定的免费刊登额度。当刊登数量超过免费额度时,才会收取每条0.3美元的刊登费。个别免费品类或产品是不包含在免费额度中的。成交费指当卖家成功售出产品后收取的费用。成交费基于买家支付的费用来计算,包含了产品费用和物流费用。在没开店铺的情况下,绝大部分产品的成交费为销售总额的10%,但最高不超过750美元。在美国站点,如果卖家的账号销售表现跌落到低于标准卖家,那么成交费的费率会有一定比例的上涨。PayPal费用包括交易手续费、提现手续费和货币兑换手续费,根据月收款额度、付款方式等条件费率有所不同。订阅店铺费是向在易贝开设店铺的卖家收取的店铺月租费,收费根据站点和店铺等级来定。特色功能费指为物品添加一些特殊功能时需要缴纳的额外费用,由卖家自主选择。

Sellers'eBay account is divided into account information and advertisement promotion. Among them, the account information is divided into three modules, including Activity, Messages and Account, as shown in Figure 2-40.

易贝的账户后台分为账号信息和商品广告推广两大部分。其中,账号信息分为三大模块,包括活动、信息和账户页面,如图2-40所示。

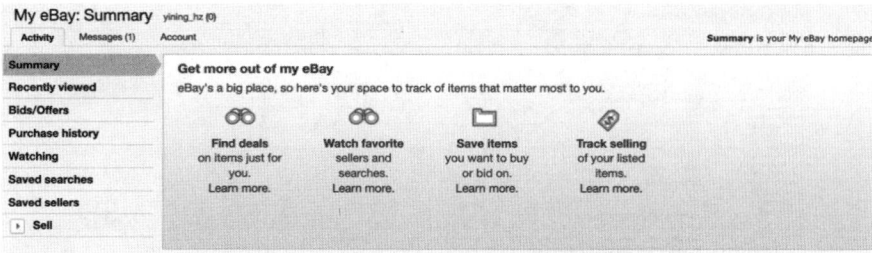

Figure 2-40 （图 2-40）

Click "Activity" to enter the account activity page, which mainly includes the user's summary of purchasing, recent browsing, shopping records, sales records and product publishing records.

点击"活动"选项,可以进入账户活动页面,该页面主要包括用户的购买摘要总结、最近浏览、购物记录、销售记录和商品刊登记录等相关信息。

Click "Messages" to go to the account information page, which mainly includes inbox, sent, draft, filing and the layout is similar to email page. Sellers can use the email signature to increase recognition. If going out for a vacation, you can turn on the out of office mode to ensure that the buyer's email gets respondence in time.

点击"信息"选项,可以进入账户信息页面,该页面主要包括收件箱、已发送、垃圾箱、存档等相关信息,类似邮箱页面。卖家可以使用邮件签名功能增加识别度,如需休假,可以开启休假模式,以确保买家的邮件及时得到反馈。

Click "Account" to go to the account page, as shown in Figure 2-41. On this page, sellers can modify their personal information, including account information, email and contact information, payment, security and social accounts. Sellers can also click on the left column to view Site Preference, Seller Dashboard, Feedback, Donation Account, Resolution Center and other information.

点击"账户"选项,可以进入账户页面,如图 2-41 所示。在该页面,卖家可以修改完善个人资料,包括修改个人账户信息、邮箱及联络信息、支付信息、安全信息和社交账号。卖家也可以点击左栏选择查看网站偏好设定、卖家成绩表、信用评价、捐款账户、调解中心等信息。

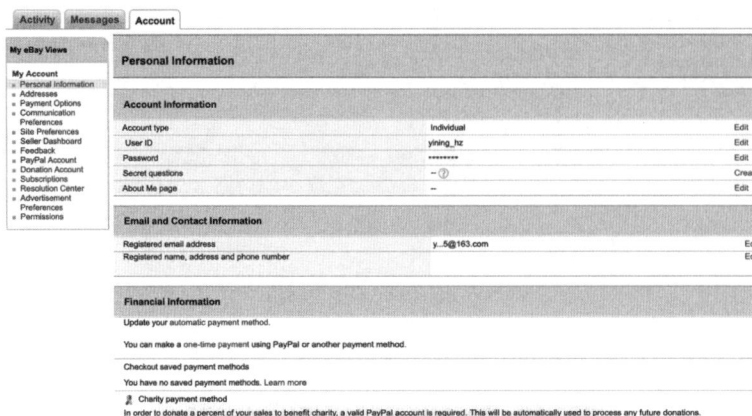

Figure 2-41（图2-41）

## Section Five / Extensive Reading: Independent Website

### 拓展阅读：独立站

An independent website means that an enterprise establishes an independent e-commerce platform for trading. Compared with third-party platforms, independent websites have the advantage of creating corporate brand image, reducing constraints of rules, and keeping all raw data. Some good examples of independent websites are LightInTheBox, Globalegrow E-Commerce, etc. However, most cross-border e-commerce export enterprises mainly sell on third-party platforms.

独立站是指企业自己建立电子商务平台进行交易。相对于第三方平台，独立站具有利于打造企业品牌形象、减少规则制约、掌握所有原始数据等优势。独立站做得比较好的企业有兰亭集势、环球易购等。但是大多数跨境电商出口企业以在第三方平台销售为主。

If enterprises need to establish independent websites, the initial cost is high. Common website building tools are Shopify, Shopyy, Ueeshop, etc. In the case of Shopify, enterprises can purchase domain names in Shopify or use their existing domain names. Shopify will provide a free myshopify.com domain name when registering. There is no charge for using the Shopify Payments provided by Shopify. Other payment methods such as PayPal, will charge a commission of 1%-2%. If an overseas consumer pays by credit card, the company will be charged accordingly by the system. With this website-building system, the cheapest option is $29 per month, with different prices for different services. Users can try Shopify for free for

14 days, which is more user-friendly.

企业建立独立站的初始成本是比较高的。常见的建站工具有 Shopify、Shopyy、Ueeshop 等。以 Shopify 为例，企业可以在 Shopify 中购买域名，也可以使用自己现有的域名。Shopify 在注册时会提供免费的 myshopify.com 域名。使用 Shopify 官方提供的 Shopify 收款是不收费的，而使用其他的收款渠道，如 PayPal，会收取 1%—2% 的佣金。海外消费者如果使用信用卡付款，企业也会被系统收取相应的费用。使用该建站系统，最便宜的方案是每月 29 美元，不同价格包含不同的服务。比较人性化的是，Shopify 可以免费试用14天。

After the independent website is set up, the core difficulty is to obtain traffic and how to operate. Different from the more mature third-party platform, independent website starts from scratch. The enterprise needs to operate on the platform and goods. The initial traffic cost is very high, and the conversion rate is crucial for the sustainable development of enterprise. Common methods of independent website to attract traffic are Facebook commercials, Google ADWORDS, KOL, remarketing, SEO, etc. After it, the enterprise should also try to increase traffic conversion. The traffic conversion can be divided into display quantity-click rate-order rate-repurchase rate, and finally form the transaction. Every aspect needs to be optimized. From display, picture design to payment design, enterprises must improve user experience and conversion rate. These all test the operational capabilities of a company.

建站完成后，独立站的核心难点在于获取流量和运营。不同于比较成熟的第三方平台，独立站是从零开始的，企业既要运营平台还要运营商品，初始的流量成本非常高，转化率的高低对于企业能否可持续发展至关重要。常见的独立站引流方式有脸书商业广告、谷歌 ADWORDS、KOL、再营销、SEO 等。引流之后，企业也要做好流量转化，流量转化可以分为展示量—点击率—下单率—复购率，最后形成交易。在每一个环节都要做优化，从展示方式、图片设计到支付设计，企业都要做好用户体验，提升转化率，这些都非常考验企业的精细化运营能力。

Adapted from www.cifnews.com（改编自雨果网）

# Chapter Three
## Cross-Border E-Commerce Marketing

跨境电商营销

## Lead-in

## 导入

In the current context of economic globalization, the competition among cross-border e-commerce enterprises is becoming increasingly fierce, and the competition for traffic is also becoming even fiercer. It is crucial for enterprises to know how to join the cross-border e-commerce wave to accurately target customers through multi-channel marketing, increase exposure, conversion rate and sales. This chapter will introduce cross-border market analysis, platform-inside marketing, social networking services (SNS) marketing, search engine optimization (SEO) and email direct marketing to help sellers understand and choose their own marketing strategies.

在当前经济全球化的大背景下,跨境电商企业间的竞争越来越激烈,流量的竞争也是日趋白热化。刚加入跨境电商浪潮的企业如何通过多渠道营销精准定位目标客户,提升曝光量、转化率和销售额显得至关重要。本章会依次介绍跨境市场分析、站内营销、社交营销、搜索引擎优化和电子邮件营销,来帮助卖家认识和选择属于自己店铺的营销策略。

## Section One / **Cross-Border Market Analysis**

## 跨境市场分析

Most cross-border e-commerce enterprises are unable to conduct market research in overseas markets due to realistic conditions. However, sellers can rely on major data analysis tools to comprehensively examine the sales of products. Sellers can use Google Trends to analyze the product's popularity of search in terms of time, region and keyword and other factors, to grasp the development trend of products. Through the use of Keywords Spy, sellers can find the popularity of the searched category and keywords. Through the use of Jungle Scout, sellers can analyze product demand and product competition on Amazon. Through the use of Terapeak, sellers can fully analyze the accounts on eBay and Amazon.

由于条件限制,大多数跨境电商企业无法到海外市场进行市场调研。但是,卖家可以依靠各大数据分析工具,全面考察商品的销售情况。卖家还可以借助谷歌趋势进行品类的时间热度、区域热度、关键词热度等分析,把握产品的发展趋势;借助 Keywords Spy 可以发现品类搜索热度和品类关键词;借助 Jungle Scout 可以分析亚马逊上产品的需求量和产品竞争程度;借助 Terapeak 可以全面分析易贝和亚马逊平台账户。

## 1. Google Trends (谷歌趋势)

Website (搜索网址): http://www.google.com/trends

Google Trends is an application based on search log analysis launched by Google. By analyzing Google's billions of search results around the world, it tells users how often the keywords are searched in Google and the relevant statistics, get the current hot content, and infer the product's low season, peak season, and search areas with high frequency of the specific keywords.

谷歌趋势是谷歌推出的一款基于搜索日志分析的应用产品。通过分析谷歌全球数以十亿计的搜索结果,告诉用户搜索某关键词各个时期在谷歌被搜索的频率和相关统计数据,得出当下热门的内容,推测出产品的淡季、旺季,以及搜索高频地区。

For example, if we search for curtains in Google Trends, we can enter curtains, curtain, blackout curtains, sheer curtains as the keywords, select the United States as the market for analysis, and set the time from May 2018 to May 2019. The results are shown in Figure 3-1. If we set the time from May 2014 to May 2019, and the results are shown in Figure 3-2. By comparing the one-year data and five-year data, it is found that the search peak of the curtain is around July, and the search time with low frequency is around December. Therefore, the sellers can choose to complete the preparation work of this product in May. Moreover, we can also see that the curtains are not seasonal products, and the overall sales data is slowly growing. The regional frequency and other related searches of curtains are shown in Figure 3-3.

例如我们在谷歌趋势搜索窗帘,输入关键词 curtains、curtain、blackout curtains、sheer curtains,选择美国作为分析市场,时间设置为2018年5月—2019年5月,显示结果如图3-1所示。如果我们把时间设置为2014年5月—2019年5月,则显示结果如图3-2所示。通过对比1年数据和5年数据,我们发现窗帘的搜索峰值在7月前后,12月前后为搜索低频期,因此产品可以选择在5月份完成备货等筹备工作。此外,我们还可以看出窗帘并非季节性产品,并且整体销售数据在缓慢增长。窗帘的地域搜索热度和相关查询如图3-3所示。

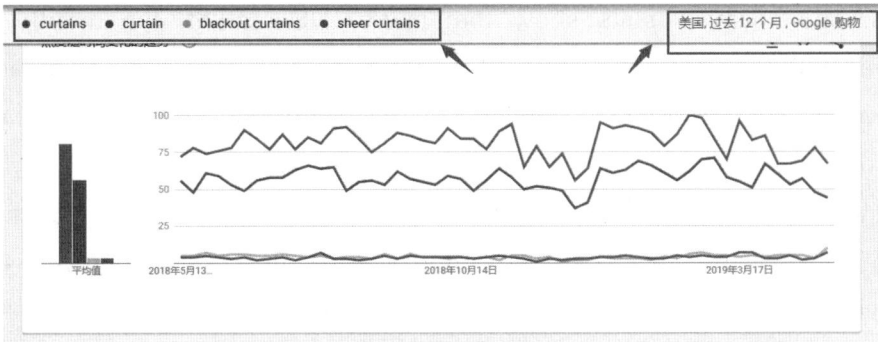

Figure 3-1（图 3-1）

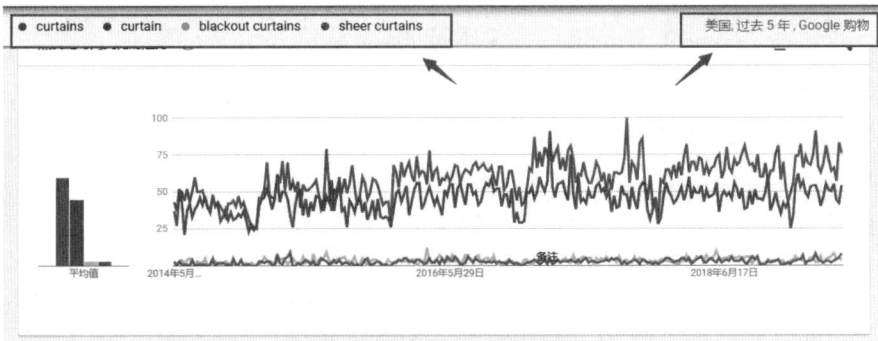

Figure 3-2（图 3-2）

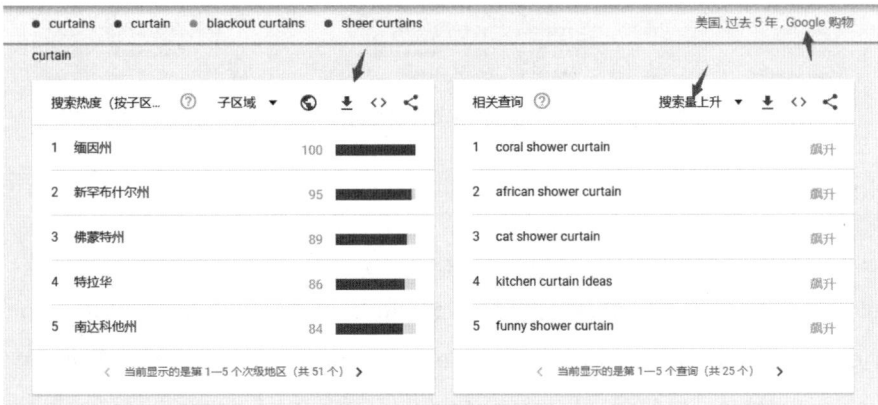

Figure 3-3（图 3-3）

## 2. KeywordSpy

Website (搜索网址): http://www.keywordspy.com

Taking curtains as an example, we enter curtains as the keyword, select the United States as the market for analysis, and select Keywords as the search condition. The search results show that in the US market, the monthly search volume reached 6.12 million, and the market is hot (see Figure 3-4). If you add other hot keywords, such as drapes, windows curtains, etc., as long tail keywords, you can improve SEO performance.

以窗帘为例,我们输入关键词curtains,选择美国为分析市场,查询条件选择关键词。搜索结果显示,在美国市场curtains月搜索量达到612万,市场热度较高(见图3-4)。如果添加其他热度比较高的关键词,如drapes、windows curtains等作为长尾关键词,可以提高SEO的优化水平。

Figure 3-4 (图3-4)

## 3. Jungle Scout

Website (搜索网址): www.junglescout.cn

Jungle Scout is a big data tool for products selection with nearly one billion Amazon catalog data. Filters can be set based on keywords, market demand (product sales), price, degree of competition (number of comments/ratings/number of sellers/listing quality), and the most promising products can be found in the largest product database. In addition, you can track your competitor's products to understand important information such as their product strategy, actual daily sales, inventory changes and some other important information.

Taking curtains as an example, we enter the keyword curtain and can get the average sales ranking, average price, average number of comments and other data (see Figure 3-5). Click on the cloud button in the lower right corner and related keywords will jump out of the box (see Figure 3-6). Click the download button to export the relevant raw data table (see Figure 3-7).

Jungle Scout是一款大数据选品工具，拥有亚马逊近10亿个产品目录数据。可以根据关键词、市场需求（产品销量）、价格、竞争程度（评论数量/评分/卖家数量/上架质量）等条件设置过滤器，在最大的产品数据库中寻找到最具潜力的产品。此外，还可以通过跟踪竞争对手的产品来了解其产品策略、每天的实际销售情况及库存变化等重要的信息。

以窗帘为例，我们输入关键词curtain，可以得到平均销售排名、平均价格、平均评论数量等数据（见图 3-5）；点击右下角云标，可以跳出相关关键词的弹框（见图 3-6）；再点击下载按钮可以导出相关的原始数据表（见图 3-7）。

Figure 3-5 （图3-5）

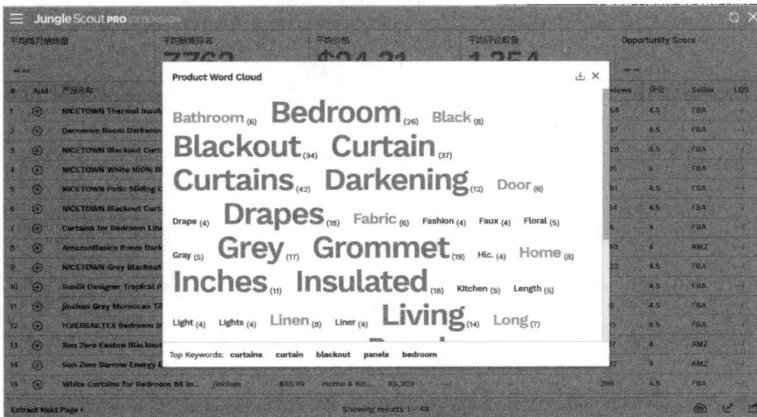

Figure 3-6 （图3-6）

Figure 3-7（图3-7）

By making a pivot table (see Figure 3-8), we can find that brands like Nicetown, Jinchan are the most popular ones, which can be used as reference and competing products for analysis.

通过制作数据透视表（见图3-8），我们可以发现集中品牌有Nicetown、Jinchan等，可作为参考对象和竞品进行分析。

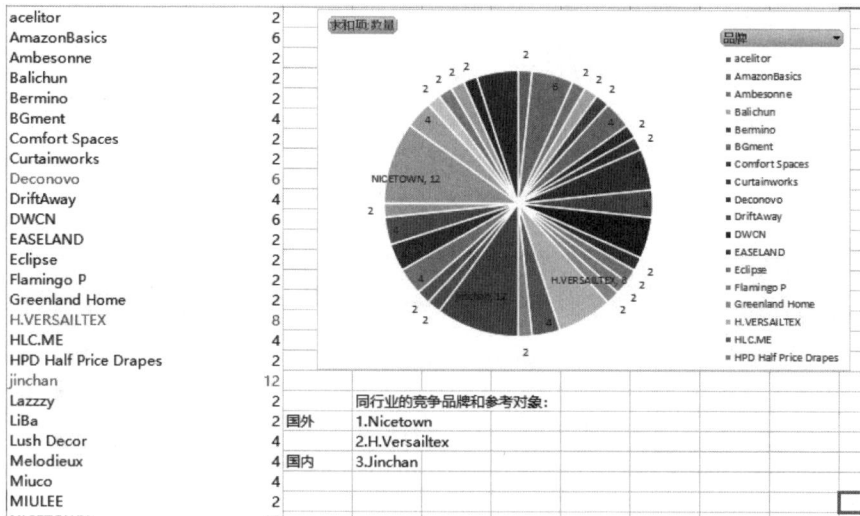

Figure 3-8（图3-8）

By analyzing products with relatively high quality and reasonable price in the price range between 18.99 and 21.99 dollars, we can find that the positive reviews of such products and the sales volume become a healthy proportional relationship. Among them, blackout curtains account for more than 65% of all research data. There are a lot of categories with many choices of colors and sizes. The inventory pressure on the side of sellers is relatively high. The prices of basic sheer curtains are relatively low, and the ones with more characteristic patterns are relatively expensive. There are currently two sizes, so the option of this product is relatively limited, and there is not so much pressure on the seller to stock up this product.

通过分析18.99—21.99美元区间性价比比较高的产品,可以发现此类产品好评数和销量成健康的正比关系。其中遮光款的数据占所有研究数据的65%以上。其品类多,颜色丰富,尺寸可选择性多,对卖家而言备货压力大;纱款的基础款价格相对较低,花纹和特性款相对售价会高一些,并且目前有两款尺寸,产品相对有限,对卖家备货压力小些。

By analyzing the high-end customized curtains in the price range of 24.99 to 38.99 dollars, there are more choices on materials and patterns. Furthermore, there are other bundles, such as Roman rods, packaging, curtain tethers, plus gauze, lighting, etc. (see Figure 3-9).

通过分析24.99—38.99美元区间的高端定制窗帘,我们发现这种窗帘有更多面料、花纹的选择,以及其他捆绑品,比如罗马杆、包装、窗帘系绳、薄纱和灯饰等(见图3-9)。

Figure 3-9 (图 3-9)

Finally, by analyzing the low price high quantity curtains in the price range of 8.99 to 14.95 dollars, it is found that these products are mostly FBA products, the profit margin is low, the negative review rate is relatively high, and there are a lot of accumulated data. There is not so much advantage if you want to compete with these products in terms of price.

最后,通过分析8.99—14.95美元的低价跑量款,我们发现这些产品多为FBA产品,利润空间小,差评率相对较高,历史累积数据高,在价格上做竞品,则优势不大。

## 4. Terapeak

Website: www.terapeak.com

搜索网址:www.terapeak.com

Terapeak was co-developed by eBay and the international public express 4PX Express, which is the only recommended market analysis tool by eBay. It helps sellers analyze eBay and Amazon accounts by integrating data from the world's two largest e-commerce platforms. The interface of Terapeak is shown in Figure 3-10. Sellers can increase market share by analyzing popular products, competitors, transaction data for similar products, and categories of popular products to better understand market conditions and then increase market share.

Terapeak 由易贝和国际速递公共平台递四方速递合作开发,是易贝官方唯一推荐的市场分析工具。它通过整合全球最大的两个电商平台数据,帮助卖家分析易贝和亚马逊平台账号。Terapeak 的界面如图 3-10 所示。卖家可以通过分析热门产品、竞争对手的情况、同类产品的交易数据,以及热门产品的类别更好地了解市场现状,从而增加市场份额。

Figure 3-10 (图 3-10)

# Section Two / **Platform-Inside Marketing**
## 站内营销

After we complete the preparation work including store registration, product selection, product information processing and uploading, and shop decoration, if we found that the data such as shop visits and product sales are still unsatisfactory, what should we do? First of all, we can use cross-border e-commerce platform-inside marketing to increase the traffic and exposure of stores and products, thereby attracting consumers and increasing sales.

当我们完成了店铺注册、选品、产品信息化处理和上传、店铺装修等前期准备工作以后，发现店铺访问量、产品销售量等数据仍然不尽人意，应该怎么办？ 首先，我们可以通过跨境电商站内营销帮助我们引流，提高店铺和产品的访问量和曝光量，从而吸引消费者，增加销量。

Platform-inside marketing, also known as platform-inside drainage, refers to sellers marketing and promotion of stores through their own marketing tools of third-party platforms, generally relying on advertising or promotion means. Platform-inside marketing needs to pay attention to platform policies, drainage rules, charging conditions, etc., pay attention to control marketing input-output ratio, and achieve profitability.

站内营销，又称站内引流，指卖家通过第三方平台自有的营销工具进行店铺的营销和推广，一般是依靠广告或促销手段。进行站内营销需要关注平台政策、引流规则、收费情况等，注意控制营销投入产出比，实现盈利。

## 1. Platform Activity（平台活动）

Platform activity is a free marketing service provided by AliExpress to sellers, which can quickly increase the exposure and click rate of a store and help sellers get a lot of free traffic. Sellers need to meet certain conditions to participate, and can register the appropriate activities in the marketing center of the platform.

平台活动是阿里巴巴速卖通向卖家提供的一项免费营销推广服务，能够快速增加店铺的曝光量、点击率，帮助卖家获得大量免费流量。卖家需要符合一定条件才能参加，可以在平台的营销中心板块选择适合的活动进行报名。

The current common platform activities include Flash Deals, Freebies, Featured Brands, Coins & Rewards, and Russian Groupon etc.

目前常见的平台活动有无线抢购活动、无线金币频道、品牌闪购、试用频道、俄罗斯团购等促销活动。

(1) Flash Deals (无线抢购活动)

Flash Deals was merged by the previous version of AliExpress Flash Deals and Super Deals. This is a platform activity that increases the traffic, brings exposure to the product, and enhances the user experience. Flash Deals is very obvious at the entrance of homepage, as shown in Figure 3-11. The hyperlink of Flash Deals is circled in the picture.

无线抢购活动是由速卖通无线抢购及 Super Deals 活动合并而成。该平台活动可提升活动流量，给产品带来曝光量，提升用户体验。无限抢购活动在首页的入口非常明显，如图 3-11 所示，用椭圆圈出的即是无限抢购的超链接。

Figure 3-11 (图 3-11)

(2) Freebies (试用频道)

The activity of Freebies provides consumers with trial opportunities of millions of high-quality Chinese products. It is one of the largest free trial center for cross-border products and the most professional global test-user sharing platform in China. At the same time, this activity also has the most comprehensive and objective trial experience report from thousands of consumers in more than 200 countries around the world, helping consumers make purchasing decisions.

试用频道为消费者提供上百万个中国优质商品的试用机会，是中国最大的跨境商品免费试用中心和最专业的全球试客分享平台之一。同时，该平台也拥有全球200多个国家的千万消费者对商品最全面、客观的试用体验报告，帮助消费者做出购买决策。

(3) Featured Brands (品牌闪购)

Featured Brands can help sellers sell products abroad and shape their brands. The platform will select one brand for each activity, and after two weeks preparation period and a three-day warm-up period, the traffic will come in within one day. As shown in Figure 3-12, whether in the warm-up period or on the day of the event, the platform will put the brand's products in the golden location of the website to ensure that the brand can reach the consumers to the greatest extent.

品牌闪购可以帮助卖家"出海"、塑造品牌形象。每场活动会选择特定的品牌,经过2周的筹备期和3天的预热期,将流量集中到一天内爆发。如图3-12所示,无论是在预热期还是活动当天,平台都会把该品牌的商品放在黄金资源位,确保品牌能够最大限度地触达消费者。

Figure 3-12 (图 3-12)

(4) Coins & Rewards (无线金币频道)

Coins & Rewards is a unique channel on mobile side. It is the channel with the highest traffic on the App and with the most sticky buyers. This channel includes a variety of gameplay and red packet offers, attracting regular return visits and subsequent conversions from global buyers. As a high-traffic marketing platform, sellers can attract more sticky buyers to their stores by setting up store coupons or signing up for full conversion of gold coins.

无线金币频道是无线端特有的频道,是目前App上流量最高、买家黏性最强的频道。该频道包括各类的游戏玩法和红包优惠,吸引着全球买家定期回访和后续转化。作为一个大流量的营销平台,卖家可以以设置店铺优惠券或者报名参加金币全额兑换商品活动的方式,吸引更多高黏度的买家到自己的店铺里购物。

(5) Russian Groupon (俄罗斯团购)

The purpose of Russian Groupon is to provide Russian speaking buyers with excellent products and services with lowest prices. The positioning is maximum flow, fastest delivery, and the best experience. Russian Groupon attaches great importance to the price of goods (merchants'supply chain capability), merchants' service capability (guaranteed service), commodity praise and sales volume.

俄罗斯团购的宗旨是提供俄语系买家极致性价比的商品和服务,定位是最大流量、最快出货和最优体验。俄罗斯团购非常重视商品的价格(商家供应链能力)、商家服务能力(服务保障)、商品好评和销量。

## 2. Store Promotions (店铺自主营销活动)

Besides platform promotions, sellers can also set up their own store promotions based on their needs, including: Product Discounts, Special Offers, Coupon, Product Bundles, and Interactive Campaigns. Before creating these five stores' own marketing activities, seller should note that the start time and end time of the event are all in US Pacific Time. Generally speaking, it is better to set the start time and end time in the prime time of foreign customers during the night, which is more likely to bring better marketing results. A combination with various marketing tools can also achieve unexpected marketing effects.

除了平台活动以外,卖家还可以根据自己的需求设置店铺自主营销活动。店铺自主营销活动包括五大营销工具:单品折扣活动、满减活动、店铺优惠券、搭配活动和互动活动。在创建这五种店铺自主营销活动前,卖家要注意活动开始时间和结束时间均为美国太平洋时间。一般来说,将开始时间和结束时间设置在国外客户所处时区的晚上黄金时段为宜,这样更容易带来比较好的营销效果。此外,联合多种营销工具也可以达到意想不到的营销效果。

(1) Product Discounts (单品折扣活动)

The activity of product discounts has the feature of full store discounts and discounts within limited time in the past. Sellers can quickly set up the activities of the whole store by "discounts according to different marketing groups". Sellers can use different discounts to promote new products, create hot sales, clear inventory, and help to increase product weight in the store. It is the seller's preferred store marketing tool. Sellers need to know the profit margin of all products before setting the discount, group all products in the store, and then choose the best discount for each group. In daily product discounts activity, the monthly limit on activity time and number is currently canceled, and the maximum length of a single event can be set up for 180 days; the activity is allowed to be suspended, the new item is allowed to be added or deleted, and the discount is allowed to be edited, which takes effect immediately. However, the platform does not allow discounted products to suspend during the time of a large-scale promotion, neither does it allow the items it to be added or deleted. And the item or shipping template is not allowed to be edited, as shown in Figure 3-13.

单品折扣活动包含了原先的全店铺打折活动和限时限量折扣的功能。卖家可以通过"按营销分组折扣"快速设置全店铺商品的活动，利用不同的折扣力度推新品、打造爆品、清库存，有利于提升产品权重，是卖家的首选店铺营销工具。卖家在设置折扣前，需要了解所有产品的利润率，先对全店铺的所有产品进行分组，再为每组选择最适合的折扣。在日常的单品折扣活动中，目前取消了每月限制的活动时长和活动次数，单场活动最长可以设置180天；允许在活动进行中暂停活动，允许新增或删除商品，以及编辑折扣，并且实时生效。但在大促场景下的单品折扣活动不允许暂停活动，不允许新增或删除商品，不允许编辑商品和运费模板。如图3-13所示。

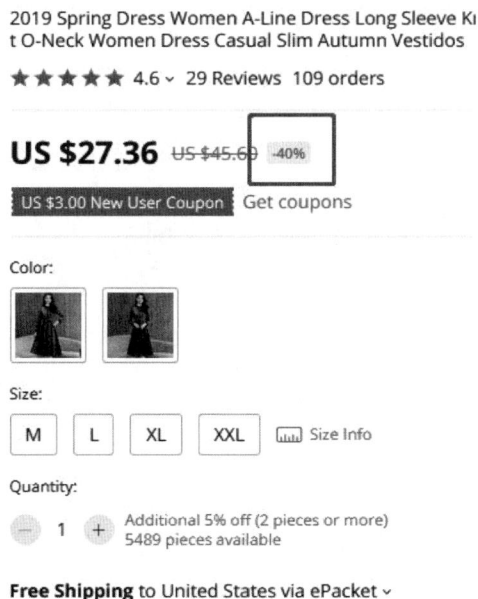

Figure 3-13 (图3-13)

(2) Special Offers (满减活动)

Special Offers include automatic special offers, special offers with a certain number of items, and free shipping with certain order amount. The purpose is to encourage buyers to buy more, increase transaction value per order. As shown in Figure 3-14, automatic special offer refers to the promotion method that the seller automatically reduces a certain amount when the order amount exceeds a certain number based on the daily order amount. Generally speaking, if you want to buy a $70 item, but only if the order amount exceeds $100, the system can reduce the amount by $20, will you buy another item in order to take part in the automatic special offer activity? Therefore, before creating the automatic special offer activity, sellers need to know how much the daily order amount is, and increase the customer's unit price and sales volume by setting the threshold for the automatic special offer to a higher level.

满减活动包括满立减、满件折和满包邮,目的都在于促使买家多买,提升客单价。如图 3-14 所示,满立减指卖家在自身客单价基础上设置订单满一定金额以后系统自动减价的促销手段。一般来说,如果要买一件 70 美元的商品,但是满立减的活动必须是购买金额在 100 美元以上系统才可以减 20 美元,那么你会不会为了满立减活动多买一件其他商品?所以在创建店铺满立减活动之前,卖家需要了解自己店铺的客单价大概是多少,然后通过设置较高的满立减的门槛,提升客单价和销量。

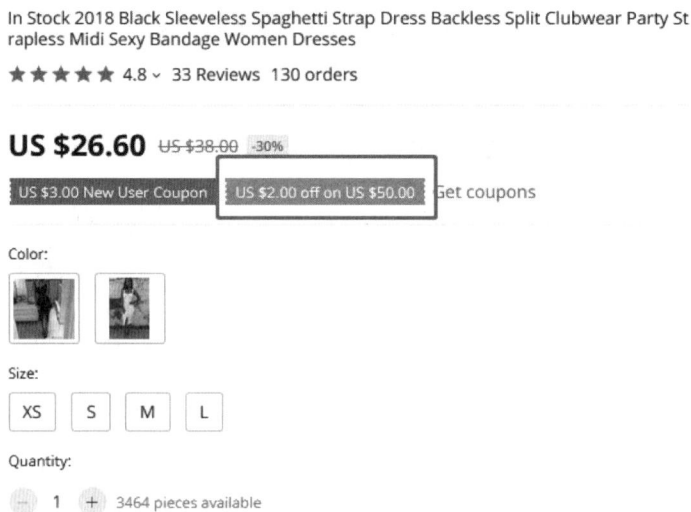

In Stock 2018 Black Sleeveless Spaghetti Strap Dress Backless Split Clubwear Party Strapless Midi Sexy Bandage Women Dresses

★ ★ ★ ★ ★ 4.8 ˅ 33 Reviews  130 orders

**US $26.60** US $38.00 -30%

US $3.00 New User Coupon | US $2.00 off on US $50.00 | Get coupons

Color:

Size:

| XS | S | M | L |

Quantity:

⊝ 1 ⊕ 3464 pieces available

Figure 3-14 (图 3-14)

Special offers with a certain number of items refers to the store's promotion rule that if you purchase X items you can get Y discount. That is, the total quantity of products equals to or exceed the number of X pieces, and when the buyer pays, he can automatically enjoy Y discount, and the seller does not need to modify the price.

满件减指对店铺设置"满 X 件优惠 Y 折"的促销规则,即订单总商品满足 X 件数,当买家付款时则享 Y 折优惠,卖家无须修改价格。

Free shipping with certain order amount refers to the promotion rule that if the order amount reaches a certain amount or pieces of products, the system automatically reduces shipping fee within the specified area when the buyer pays.

满包邮指卖家在店铺设置"满 N 元/件包邮"的促销规则。买家下单时,若是订单超过了设置的价格或件数,在买家付款时,在指定的地区范围内,系统自动减免邮费。

(3) Coupon (店铺优惠券)

Coupon is a store marketing tool that is set by the seller to set the discount amount and use conditions, and the buyer uses it within the valid period. Store coupons are divided into click-to-have coupons, targeted coupons, and interactive coupons.

店铺优惠券是由卖家自主设置优惠金额和使用条件,买家领取后在有效期内使用的店铺营销工具。店铺优惠券分为领取型优惠券、定向发放型优惠券和互动型优惠券。

Click-to-have coupons are issued through various channels, including platform-inside messages, social media and other channels. After users obtain the coupons, they can purchase with them. Click-to-have coupons are effective means of external drainage, conversion and developing new customers. And the prices paid will not be included in the historical lowest price. The seller can click on "Marketing Campaign" in the seller's dashboard, select "Coupon" under "Store Activity", and click "Create Activity".

领取型优惠券通过各种渠道发放,包括站内信、社交媒体等渠道,用户获取后到店购买使用,是站外引流、转化、拉新的有效手段,而且不计入历史最低价。卖家可以在速卖通后台点击"营销活动",在"店铺活动"选择"店铺优惠券",点击"创建活动"。

Targeted coupons are directly sent to certain customers. Any buyer who has purchased in store, added products to a shopping cart or a wish list can be selected for targeted marketing. The seller only needs to create a coupon activity, select the object to be distributed, and click "Send" to issue coupons to new and returning customers. Targeted coupons are divided into "direct distribution" and "QR code distribution".

定向发放型优惠券指向指定用户发放的优惠券,凡是与店铺有过交易、将商品加到购物车或者愿望清单的买家都可作为定向发放对象,用于定向营销。卖家只需创建优惠券活动,选择发放对象,点击发放,即可利用优惠券激活新老买家。定向发放型优惠券分为"直接发放"和"二维码发放"两种。

Interactive coupons include gold coin coupons, flash coupons and popular coupons. The gold coin coupon means that the buyer can obtain gold coins through signing in on the App, planting a tree and other tasks. They can convert the gold coins into coupons, and then use them in certain stores. Flash coupons can help sellers attract buyers to the store through large-value store coupons without thresholds, which can effectively increase buyer interests. A popular coupon means that the buyer can quickly bring new traffic to the store by sharing the invitation with others.

互动型优惠券包括金币兑换优惠券、秒抢优惠券和聚人气优惠券。金币兑换优惠券指买家通过登录App签到、种树等任务获得金币,兑换成优惠券,然后在兑换优惠券的店里使用。秒抢优惠券指卖家通过无门槛的大额店铺优惠券吸引买家到店,可有效提高买家的活跃度。聚人气优惠券指通过买家分享邀请他人的方式快速给店铺带来新流量。

(4) Product Bundles (搭配活动)

Product Bundles refer to the combination sales of store products, which can improve conversion rate and increase order amount per customer. The new version of product bundles is that the seller can edit bundles created by the algorithm, and decide prices independently. Sellers can select 1 main item and no more than four affiliate items, and set the bundle price at the same time. A product can be used as the main item in up to three bundle packages, and can be used as an affiliate item in 100 bundle packages.

搭配活动指将店铺商品进行组合销售,可以刺激转化,提高客单价。在新版搭配活动中,卖家可以编辑算法来创建搭配套餐,并进行自主定价。卖家可选择1个主商品和1—4个子商品,同时设置搭配价。一个商品最多可作为主商品在3个搭配套餐中,最多可作为子商品在100个搭配套餐中。

(5) Interactive Activities (互动活动)

Interactive Activities are divided into two categories: interactive games and group buying. Sellers can set up three interactive games: Flip and Win, Bubble Challenge, and Add to Cart, where event time, buyers' interactions, and gifts can be set all by sellers themselves. Then put them into the fan posts after setting, which can quickly attract traffic to the store. Group buying is a tool that can quickly attract new customers, set a lower discount through group marketing tool, and drive users to share with their friends and place more orders.

店铺互动活动分为互动游戏和拼团两类。卖家可设置"翻牌子""打泡泡"和"收藏有礼"三种互动游戏,其中活动时间、买家互动次数和奖品都可自行设置,设置后放入粉丝趴帖子中可快速吸引流量到店。拼团是一个可以快速、拉新用户的工具,其通过拼团营销工具设置较低的折扣,驱动用户在站外和好友分享并共同下单。

## 3. Affiliate Marketing（联盟营销）

Affiliate marketing, usually referred to as online affiliate marketing, is an online marketing method that pays for marketing performance. That is, merchants use the website alliance service provided by professional affiliate marketing agencies to expand their online and offline businesses, and expand sales space and channels. And it is a new online marketing mode that pays according to marketing performance. Affiliate marketing is one of the largest overseas network alliance systems in China. It is a relatively effective channel for novice sellers to promote their store and quickly increase exposure.

联盟营销,通常是指网络联盟营销,是一种按营销效果付费的网络营销方式,即商家利用专业联盟营销机构提供的网站联盟服务拓展其线上及线下业务,扩大销售空间和销售渠道,并按照营销实际效果支付费用的新型网络营销模式。联盟营销是国内最大的海外网络联盟体系之一,是新手卖家营销推广、快速提升流量曝光的一个比较有效的渠道。

AliExpress sellers can freely set commission rates within the range of 3%–50% through "My AliExpress"—"Marketing" to join affiliate marketing. If the seller receives the order through affiliate marketing channel, the commission will be paid according to the proportion of the transaction, which is set in advance. After participating in the affiliate marketing program, in addition to the existing exposure, the store will receive additional exposure in AliExpress's exclusive channel, and will receive massive alliance traffic outside the station, covering hundreds of countries and billions of overseas buyers around the world, accurately matching the region and shopping habits. Sellers participating in affiliate marketing do not need to pay any fees in advance, and the promotion process is completely free.

速卖通卖家可以通过"我的速卖通"中的"营销中心",在规定的3%—50%范围内自由设置佣金比例,加入联盟营销。如果卖家通过联盟营销渠道收到了订单,则需按照事先自己设定的交易比例来支付佣金。加入联盟营销之后,商品除了现有的曝光外,在站内会在速卖通的联盟专属频道得到额外曝光,在站外会得到海量联盟流量,覆盖全球上百个国家和数十亿海外买家,精准匹配地域和购物习惯。参与联盟营销的卖家无须预先支付任何费用,推广过程完全免费。

(1) Location of Affiliate Marketing (联盟展示位置)

There will be two locations for products that join affiliate marketing, inside the platform and outside the platform. In the station, buyers can search for goods by keyword and category. The system will display and recommend products based on the browsing history and purchasing behavior. Outside the station, the products may be in three channels: global network (such as Google and other search engines, Facebook and other social networking sites, YouTube and other video sites), regional network alliances (such as Admitad in Russia, Awin in Europe and other regional alliances) and local media.

加入联盟营销的商品会基于站内和站外两块分别展示。在站内,买家可以按照关键词、类目搜索商品,系统会基于买家历史的浏览和采购行为千人千面地展示和推荐商品;在站外,商品会在全球性的网络(如谷歌等搜索引擎、脸书等社交网站和YouTube等视频网站)、区域性的网盟(如俄罗斯的Admitad、欧洲的Awin等区域一级联盟)和本地的媒体三种渠道上展示。

(2) Ranking Rules of Affiliate Marketing (联盟排序规则)

There are mainly three ranking rules of affiliate marketing. ① Alliance traffic position (best.aliexpress.com) and the product listing page will rank the products based on multiple dimensions. The overall score will include whether it is hot, its commission rate, historical sales, etc. ② On Alliance traffic position (best.aliexpress.com), if products have the same website comprehensive score, the higher the commission rate, the higher the ranking. ③ On the main website of AliExpress (www.aliexpress.com), the sales of the Alliance are weighted in the main search.

联盟排序主要依靠以下三个规则。①联盟流量阵地(best.aliexpress.com)和商品展示页,会基于多个维度综合得分来排序,其中包含是否爆品、佣金比例、历史销量等。②联盟流量阵地(best.aliexpress.com),商品在同等的网站综合得分下,佣金比例越高则排序越靠前。③速卖通网站主站(www.aliexpress.com),联盟的销量享有主搜加权。

(3) Payment Rules of Affiliate Marketing (联盟付费规则)

If buyer clicks on the advertisement link of the product promoted by affiliate marketing and the order is placed within 15-day tracking valid period, this order will be judged as the order brought by the alliance, and the alliance commission will be charged after the transaction is completed. Affiliate marketing commission fee = merchandise turnover (excluding shipping) × merchandise commission rate (commission rate when placing the order).

如果买家点击了联盟推广出去的商品的广告链接，且在15天的追踪有效期内下单，那么会被判断为是联盟带来的订单，交易成功后卖家会被收取联盟佣金。联盟佣金费用=商品成交金额（不含运费）×商品佣金比例（下单时的佣金比例）。

## Section Three / SNS Marketing
## 社交营销

In addition to platform-inside marketing, the marketing approaches we use to increase traffic from other websites to cross-border e-commerce stores are called platform-outside marketing. In terms of platform-outside marketing approaches, SNS marketing plays an essential role in attracting off-site traffic and improving conversion rate of websites and stores.

除了站内营销之外，我们将通过其他网站引流到跨境电商店铺的营销方式称为站外营销。在站外营销方式中，社交营销对于网站及店铺的站外引流和转化起着至关重要的作用。

SNS (Social Networking Services), also referred to as Social Network Software, includes social software and social networking sites. It refers to websites and technologies that allow people to write, share, evaluate, discuss, and communicate with each other, which is a platform for producing and exchanging the content based on user's relationship on the Internet. The essence of socialization is sharing and interaction, and SNS marketing refers to a way to use marketing social networks, online communities, blogs or other Internet collaboration platform media to develop marketing, public relations and customer service. Due to the limited traffic in the platform, the cost of paid traffic is getting higher and higher, and social media marketing has the advantages of low cost, high reach, easy to build brands, and is often used as a way to increase traffic in cross-border e-commerce.

SNS（社交网络服务），也指社交网络软件，包括社交软件和社交网站，是指允许人们撰写、分享、评价、讨论、相互沟通的网站和技术，是互联网上基于用户关系的内容生产与交换的平台。社交的本质是分享互动，而社交营销即利用社会化网络、在线社区、博客或者其他互联网协作平台媒体来进行营销、公共关系和客户服务维护开拓的一种方式。由于目前平台站内流量有限,付费流量成本越来越高,而社交媒体营销具有低成本、高触及率、易打造品牌等优势,常常被作为跨境电商引流的方式。

In recent years, the ways of socialization provided by SNS have become increasingly humanized. More and more consumers are fond of shopping on social platforms such as Facebook and Instagram, and the proportion of shopping directly in e-commerce platform stores is getting lower and lower. Cross-border e-commerce sellers are now increasing their efforts in marketing and promoting products and brands on Facebook and Instagram, allowing consumers to make purchases directly on the social platform. The most representative social media platforms in the world include Facebook, Instagram, Pinterest, YouTube, LinkedIn and so on.

近年来,社交网络服务提供的社交方式越来越人性化,越来越多的消费者青睐于使用脸书和照片墙等社交平台购物,在卖家的电商平台店铺购物的比重越来越低。现在跨境电商卖家也越来越多地在脸书和社交网络服务营销和推广产品及品牌,让消费者可以直接在平台上进行购买。国际上最具代表性的社交媒体平台包括脸书、社交网络服务、拼趣、优兔和领英等。

## 1. Facebook 脸书 (www.facebook.com)

Facebook was founded by Zuckerberg in February 2004. Since its launch, after more than a decade of development, it has already owned nearly 2.3 billion MAU and 94% of its traffic is concentrated on the mobile side. It is currently the world's largest social network. According to Alexa's comprehensive website ranking, Facebook's website traffic and visitors ranked Top3 among all global websites. Facebook's fundamental goal is to "help people connect with friends in life". It is a versatile platform, so there is nothing particularly unsuitable for selling. Of course, if sellers are targeting at Russian market, they should choose VK instead of Facebook.

脸书是由扎克伯格在2004年2月创建的。自上线以来,经过十几年的发展,其已经拥有近23亿月活用户,94%流量集中在移动端,是目前全球最大的社交网络。根据Alexa的网站综合排名,脸书的网站流量、访客数均位列全球网站前三名。脸书的基本定位是"帮人们连接生活中的朋友",是一个百搭平台,因此没什么特别不适合卖的品类。当然,如果面向俄罗斯市场,卖家应该选择VK而非脸书。

Facebook is divided into two types of pages: personal pages and company pages. If cross-border e-commerce sellers want to promote their own stores and products through Facebook, first they need to register a Facebook account on the official website. Facebook adopts the real-name system. When registering, it must ensure the authenticity and accuracy of all information. When the account is restricted or blocked, users can get back the account through a valid ID card and other valid documents. In addition to personal accounts, sellers can also register a Facebook Page for their store. Sellers can interact with fans through the public homepage to improve customers' stickiness. The login page for Facebook is shown in Figure 3-15.

脸书分为两类页面：个人页面和公司页面。跨境电商商家想要通过脸书推广自己的店铺和产品，首先需要在官网注册一个脸书账号。脸书采取实名制，注册时一定要保证信息的真实性和准确性，便于账号受限或封锁时通过身份证等有效证件申诉要回账号。除了个人账号，卖家也可以为自己的店铺注册一个公共主页。卖家可以通过公共主页与粉丝进行良好的互动，提高客户黏性。脸书的登录页面如图3-15所示。

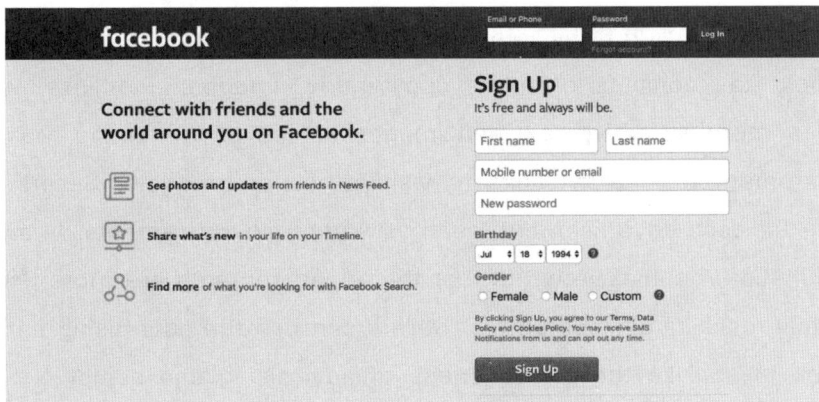

Figure 3-15 (图3-15)

Facebook's operational skills include the following: ①Maintain 4-5 posts per day, combined with performance analysis tools to find out the online active time of fans. ② Posting content generally covers product (popular hot sales) and non-product (fan related topics, open discussion topics, hot topics, etc.). ③ Post various forms of contents, including pictures, videos, live broadcasts, coupons, etc. ④ Cross-publish to enrich content and expand audiences, as well as achieve win-win cooperation. ⑤ Maintain existing fans and respond in a timely manner.

脸书的运营技巧包括：①保持每天发布4—5个帖子的频率，结合成效分析工具，找出粉丝在线活跃时间节点。②发帖内容一般涵盖产品帖（流行热卖款）和非产品帖（粉丝相关话题、开放性话题、时下热门话题等）。③发帖形式多样，包括图片、视频、直播、优惠等。④交叉发布，丰富内容，拓展受众群体，合作共赢。⑤维护现有粉丝，及时回复信息。

When posting content, you should be aware of: ① Don't reveal user's privacy. Don't identify or imply personal characteristics of the user: name, race, ethnicity, sexual preference, physical disability, mental retardation or magnified defects, implied discrimination, etc. ② Never use false exaggeration statements, including errors, fraud, misleading activities, as well as exaggerate product effects and promotional activity. ③ Don't illegally land a link outside the advertiser's own website.

在发布内容时，要注意：①不泄露用户隐私，即不指明或暗示用户个人特征：姓名、种族、族裔、性取向、身体残疾、智力障碍或者放大缺陷、隐含歧视等。②杜绝虚假夸张陈述，包括错误、欺诈、误导、夸张产品效果及活动力度等。③不非法着陆到广告主自身网站以外的链接。

The main paid promotion methods of Facebook are Facebook Ads and Promote Post.

脸书付费推广的主要方式为Facebook Ads和Promote Post。

Facebook Ads consists of titles, copywriting, images, and links. It generally uses simpler, more attractive text and images to convey marketing messages and attracts customers to click on links to visit stores or products. Sellers can set a target group for each advertisement, such as setting advertisements by age, gender, region, occupation, hobbies, etc., so that the advertisements are more accurate and can accurately reach target customers. Sellers can use the advertising data provided by Facebook to analyze the effectiveness of advertising and adjust our marketing strategy in time.

Facebook Ads由标题、文案、图片和链接组成，一般用较为简洁、有吸引力的文字和图片来传达营销信息，并吸引客户点击链接访问店铺或产品。卖家可以为每条广告设置目标人群，比如通过年龄、性别、地域、职业、兴趣爱好等条件来设置广告，使广告投放更精准，能够准确触达目标客户。卖家可以通过脸书提供的广告数据来分析广告投放的效果，并及时调整营销策略。

In addition, sellers can also promote our products or stores through personal accounts or Facebook Page postings. Sellers can promote any of the posts, as well as setting the target audience they want to reach and daily promotion budget. This is a more convenient and low-cost way to promote on Facebook, but it can bring positive results.

除此之外，卖家还可以通过个人账号或在脸书商户专页发帖来宣传和推广自己的产品或店铺。卖家可以对任意一则帖子进行推广，同样也可以设置其想要触及的目标人群，以及每日的推广预算。这是一种较为便捷和低成本的脸书推广方式，但能带来不错的效果。

## 2. Instagram（www.instagram.com）

Instagram was founded in October 2010 by Kevin Systrom and Mike Krieger. It was originally run on iOS and is the originator of image social media software. In 2012, Instagram was acquired by Facebook for $1 billion, when there were only 13 employees and about 30 million users. At present, Instagram has 1 billion monthly users, and it is still growing rapidly.

Instagram 是由凯文·斯特罗姆和麦克·克里格于 2010 年 10 月创立的，最初运行于 iOS，是图片社交媒体软件的鼻祖。2012 年，Instagram 被脸书以 10 亿美元收购，当时仅有 13 名员工，约 3000 万用户。目前 Instagram 拥有 10 亿月活用户，而且还在持续快速增长中。

Users who use Instagram are mainly young women, and users below 35 years old account for up to 90%. The ecology of online celebrities is complete on Instagram. More than 50% of millennials believe that Instagram has the biggest influence on their online shopping choices. Facebook ranks second with just over 30% of the vote, while Twitter only gets 10% of the millennials. It can be said that Instagram is the most influential social media for young people. Therefore, for businesses in fashion, women, pets, home and maternal, child industries, Instagram is an effective marketing platform.

使用 Instagram 的用户以年轻女性为主，35 岁以下的用户占比高达 90%，线上网红生态系统完整。超过 50% 的千禧一代认为，Instagram 对他们网购选择商品的影响力最大，脸书以刚过 30% 的投票率位列第二，而推特只得到了 10% 的千禧一代的青睐。可以说，Instagram 是对年轻人来说最具影响力的社交媒体。所以，对于时尚、女性、宠物、家居和母婴等行业的商家来说，Instagram 是一个有效的营销平台。

Instagram's operation is very simple, you can log in with your Facebook account or you can register your account separately. Instagram login page is shown in Figure 3-16. Users post beautiful pictures with short text, while others are free to like, comment and share. In addition to the posts posted by friends, users can also see their friends' moments, including who the friends are following, which posts they like, which posts they have commented on, and so on. Since Instagram doesn't allow any links to appear in the post, the bio at the profile page becomes the only place where we can put the store link. Remember to write "Click the Link in My Bio" in each post to remind customers to purchase products by clicking on the link on their homepage.

Instagram 的操作非常简单，用户可以用脸书账号登录也可以单独注册账号。Instagram 的登录页面如图 3-16 所示。用户发布精美的图片加上简短的文字，而其他人可以自由地点赞、评论和分享。除了好友发布的帖子，用户还可以看到他们的好友动态，包括好友关注了谁、给哪个帖子点了赞、评论了哪个帖子等等。由于 Instagram 不允许在帖子中出现任何链接，所以个人主页处的个人简介成了唯一可以放入店铺链接的地方。卖家需记得在每一个宣传帖子里写上"Click the Link in My Bio"等句子，提醒客户可以通过点击个人主页的链接购买产品。

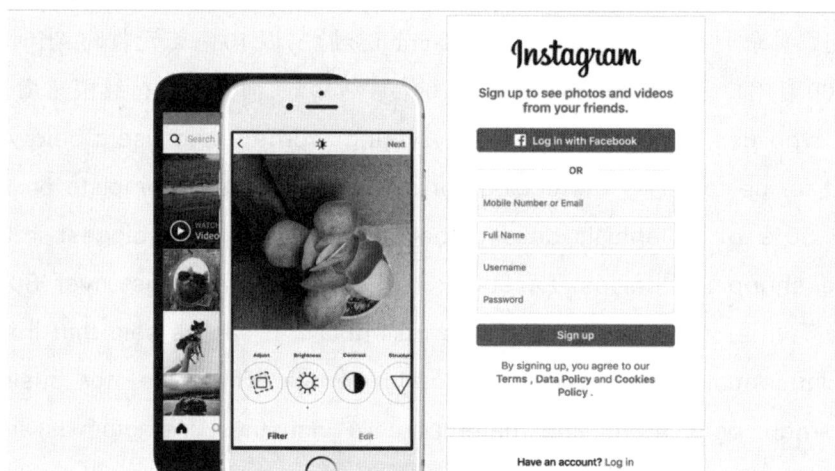

Figure 3-16 (图 3-16)

Since Instagram is a photo sharing platform, the quality of the image directly affects the exposure and click rate of the post. The photos sellers post on Instagram must be beautiful and attractive, so that their products can stand out. The color of the picture should suit brand style, maintain consistency and enhance brand recognition. Bright patterns are more popular than gray ones and can get more than 24% like. It is more attractive to put pictures with more blue color than red color, and can get more than 24% like. Monotones are more popular than multi-tones, and the number of likes increases at a rate of 17%.

由于 Instagram 是一个图片分享平台，图片的质量直接影响帖子的曝光率和点击率。卖家发布在 Instagram 的照片一定要精美，具有吸引力，让产品能够脱颖而出。图片色调要适合品牌风格，保持一致性，提高品牌的辨识度。明亮的图案比灰暗的图片更受欢迎，能得到多于24%的赞。蓝色主调的图片比红色主调的图片更吸引人，能得到多于24%的赞。单色调比多色调更受人喜爱，点赞数以17%的速率增长。

Instagram users will search for content of interest through hashtags. Sellers must use hashtags to attract traffic when posting contents, so that more people will pay attention to posts. The format of the hashtag is "#+Keyword". Sellers can use the hashtags to exactly describe the product, or use some trendy, popular hashtags. There can be no spaces between words. There should not be too many hashtags of each post. It is more appropriate to choose about 4 hashtags.

Instagram用户会通过标签来搜索感兴趣的内容，所以卖家在发布帖子时一定要巧用标签来引流，使更多人关注到帖子。标签的格式是"#+关键词"，卖家可以使用精准定位产品的标签，或是使用一些时髦、受欢迎的标签，各个词之间不能有空格。一个帖子的标签不宜过多，选择4个左右的标签较为合适。

The following marketing tools can also be used on Instagram: ① Ask fans before developing new products, let fans decide the best solution by the number of likes and comments, and improve customer loyalty and satisfaction. ② Hold lottery or picture contest, and set prizes to attract more fans to participate in order to strengthen fan interaction. According to the survey, more than 70% of Instagram users are keen to participate in various brand competitions. ③ Give fans some benefits, coupons or internal information. 41% of Instagram users say they will pay more attention to brands that give fans discounts or small giveaways.

Instagram还有以下一些营销手段：①在开发新产品前询问粉丝意见，让粉丝通过点赞数和评论数决定最佳方案，提升客户忠诚度和满意度。②举办抽奖或是图片比赛，设置一些奖品来吸引更多的粉丝参与，加强粉丝互动。根据调查显示，超过70%的Instagram用户热衷于参加各种各样的品牌比赛。③给粉丝一些福利、优惠券或者内部消息。41%的Instagram用户称，他们会关注那些给予粉丝优惠或者小赠品的品牌。

## 3. Pinterest (www.pinterest.com) 拼趣

In March 2010, Pinterest was founded by Ben Silbermann, Paul Sciarra and Evan Sharp. It is a media software and is the originator of the "Waterfall Stream" display image. Pinterest currently has 250 million monthly users, aged between 25 and 55. It is a paradise for housewives, especially European and American housewives. The shared content is mainly life related and the most popular contents include home, gardening, beauty, health and food. The login page of Pinterest is shown in Figure 3-17.

拼趣成立于2010年3月,由本·希尔伯曼、保罗于·斯艾拉和伊文·夏普共同创立,也是一款图片社交媒体软件,是"瀑布流"展示图片的鼻祖。拼趣目前拥有月活用户2.5亿,年龄从25岁到55岁。拼趣是家庭主妇的天堂,尤其受欧美主妇的欢迎。拼趣用户分享的内容以生活类为主,家居、园艺、美妆、健康和美食是最受欢迎的几类内容。拼趣的登录页面如图3-17所示。

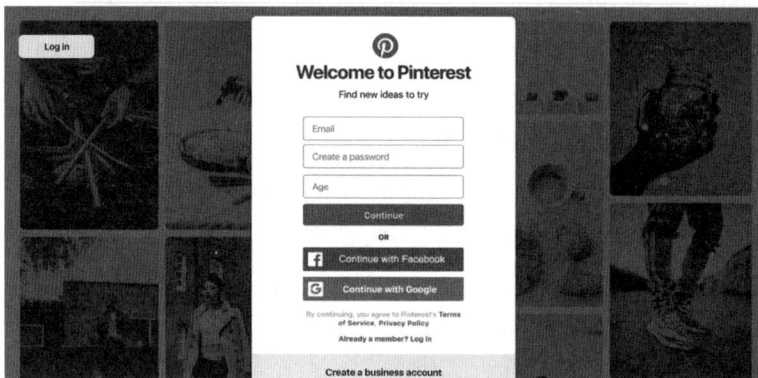

Figure 3-17 (图3-17)

Pinterest is inspired by Pin plus Interest, where users collect content of interest and pin them to a board. Pin can be understood as a picture or video that is posted on the board by users. That is, users collect their favorite picture or video, and the board is a group of pictures or videos, similar to the album that we are familiar with. Like other social media, users can like and comment on content that they have interests in, or they can post these contents to their own board via Repin. Users can also add a source to the image or video, that is, the URL of the image or video source. Other users can directly click to enter the website to browse and purchase.

拼趣的灵感来源于pin加上interest,即用户搜集感兴趣的内容,并把它们"钉"在一个白板上。pin可以理解为被用户贴在板上的图片或视频,也就是用户收集喜欢的图片或视频,而白板也就是一个图片或视频的集合,类似于我们熟知的相册。像其他社交媒体一样,用户可以给感兴趣的内容点赞和评论,也可以通过"重钉"把它贴到自己的板上。用户还可以给图片或视频加上标示来源的网址,其他用户可以直接点击进入网站进行浏览和购买。

Pinterest is a high-purchase platform with an average purchase rate of around 15%, mainly in facial and body care, fashion styles (fashion and accessories), health products, home and garden, cooking and food. The facial and body care purchase rate is as high as 16.8%, which is much higher than 12.6% of other social platforms.

拼趣是一个购买率很高的平台,平均购买率为 15% 左右,主要表现在面部和身体护理、时尚风格(时装与饰品)、健康产品、家和花园、烹饪与美食等品类。其中面部和身体护理购买率高达 16.8%,远远高于其他社交平台的 12.6%。

The following marketing tips can be used on Pinterest: ① Improve the portrait and profile to make it fit the product positioning. A "Pin It" button can be added to the store's homepage to make it easy for fans to post sellers' content to the Pinterest board. Etsy, the American crafts e-commerce site, has added the "Pin It" button to its website. For small businesses that do business with a large number of Internet users, it is important for potential users to find these sites quickly. ② Optimize the picture and board, build a few more boards according to the content, and release pictures that are interesting and can attract viewers. In addition, since text matching comes first in the search mechanism of Pinterest, the board must contain keywords that are more likely to be searched. ③ Create Pins that are related to hot topics, or engage in interesting content from other active Repin users, which both can bring sellers more attention and fans. ④ Similar to Instagram, sellers can also hold lottery or competition to interact with fans better, increase attention and increase user's stickiness.

拼趣还有以下一些营销手段:①首先完善头像和简介,使之符合自身产品定位。可以在店铺首页增加一个"Pin It"的按钮,以方便粉丝能够将卖家的内容发布到拼趣白板当中。美国工艺品电子商务网站 Etsy 就已经在自家网站上增加了"Pin It"按钮。对于面向大量网民开展业务的小型商家而言,潜在用户能否快速找到这些网站至关重要。②优化图片和白板,按内容多建几个白板,发布有意思、能吸引浏览量的图片。除此之外,由于拼趣搜索机制中以文字匹配优先,所以白板中必须包含可能被搜索到的关键词。③创建与热门话题相关的 Pins,或是积极 Repin 其他用户有意思的内容,都能为卖家带来更多的关注和粉丝。④和 Instagram 类似,卖家也可以通过举办抽奖或比赛,来更好地与粉丝互动,增加关注,提高用户黏性。

## 4. YouTube (www.youtube.com)

Founded in February 2005, YouTube was established by Chad Hurley, Steven Chen, and Jawed Karim as a video-sharing site. In October 2006, Google acquired YouTube for $1.65 billion and operated it as a subsidiary company. YouTube currently has more than 1.9 billion monthly users, of which 1.5 billion are daily users from 73 countries and regions. The coverage is high and 71% of the US online population use YouTube. Moreover, every user watches an average of 72 videos per month, and the stickiness of users is very high. YouTube is suitable for online services and 3C products, and it is also suitable for online celebrity marketing.

YouTube 成立于 2005 年 2 月，由查德·贺利、陈士骏、贾德·卡林姆共同创办，是一个视频分享网站。2006 年 10 月，谷歌以 16.5 亿美元收购了 YouTube 网站，并把其当成一家子公司来经营。YouTube 目前月活跃用户超过 19 亿，其中有 15 亿是日活跃用户，来自 73 个国家和地区；YouTube 的覆盖度高，71% 的美国在线人口都使用它，并且每个用户每个月平均收看 72 条视频，用户黏性高。YouTube 适合投放线上服务和 3C 类产品的广告，也适合网络红人营销。

Before create a YouTube account, sellers must have a Google account, or they can log in with their Google accounts as YouTube account. The home page of YouTube is shown in Figure 3-18. If sellers want to upload a video, post a comment, or create a playlist, they can create a public YouTube channel. Sellers can customize the channel to reflect the brand identity, such as uploading profiles and cover photos, adding company descriptions, emails, and puting relevant links on the cover to give other users a better understanding of their own information.

创建 YouTube 账户前，卖家必须要有谷歌账户，其也可以用谷歌账户作为 YouTube 账户登录。YouTube 的首页如图 3-18 所示。如果想要上传视频、发表评论或制作播放列表，卖家可以创建一个公开的 YouTube 频道，并自定义频道来反映品牌标识。卖家可以上传个人资料和封面照片，添加公司说明、邮箱，并将相关链接放到封面上，使其他用户更好地了解自己的信息。

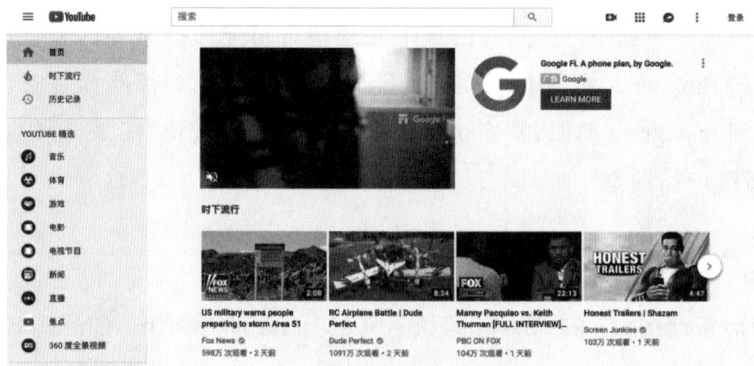

Figure 3-18 (图 3-18)

YouTube also has some of the following marketing tools: ① Focus on and take advantage of the "How-to" channel to understand fans' needs. For example, through communicating with some consumers and market research, UNice found that there are two main appeals in the target market. Thus, they attracted the attention of fans by making corresponding videos. Appeal 1: Going to the hair salon is too expensive, and it is too difficult to wear a wig. What should I do? Solution: Publish the How-to video to teach users to easily use UNice products at home. Appeal 2: Users are eager to get guidance on popular hairstyle. Solution: Use a variety of product sample videos to tell users what hairstyles are most popular right now. ② Find online celebrities and let them represent or promote it. According to the number of fans, the online celebrities are divided into different levels. It isn't true that the promotional effect is always better with higher rank online celebrity. The seller should consider the position of online celebrities and its own products, as well as budget, to choose the appropriate online celebrities to represent the brand or for promotion. The purpose is to increase brand communication and popularity.

YouTube还有以下一些营销手段：①关注并利用好"如何"频道，了解粉丝需求。比如，UNice通过与一部分消费者沟通和市场调查，发现目标市场主要有两大诉求，于是，他们就通过制作相对应的视频，吸引粉丝的持续关注。诉求1：去理发店做发型太贵了，自己戴假发又太难，怎么办？解决办法：发布How-to视频，教用户在家轻轻松松自己用UNice产品做造型。诉求2：用户渴望获得流行的发型指导。解决办法：用各种产品示例视频告诉用户现在最流行什么发型。②找网红代言或推广。按照粉丝数，网红被分为不同等级，但并不是等级越高的网红传播效果就越好。卖家可以结合网红和自身产品定位及预算，选择合适的网红进行代言或推广，增加品牌传播力度和知名度。

## 5. LinkedIn （www.linkedin.com）（领英）

Founded in December 2002 by Reid Hoffman, LinkedIn is the world's largest professional social networking site and a social network for business customers. LinkedIn currently has 450 million users, and monthly users account for only 25%. In June 2016, Microsoft announced the acquisition of LinkedIn for $26.2 billion in cash.

领英由雷德·霍夫曼于2002年12月创立，是全球最大的职业社交网站，同时是一家面向商业客户的社交网络公司。领英拥有4.5亿用户，月活跃用户仅占到25%。2016年6月，微软宣布以262亿美元收购领英公司。

LinkedIn users are mostly professional people in various fields, company bosses or staff, freelancers, etc. It is essential to establish connections with these people to expand cross-border e-commerce business, especially for B2B business. Sellers can also learn the most comprehensive industry trends through industry news published by overseas distributors, including getting to know the fashion trends, shopping trends, and consumer trends in target countries.

领英的用户大多是各个领域的专业人士、公司老板或职员、自由职业者等,通过与这些人脉建立联系,对拓展跨境电商业务,尤其对B2B业务至关重要。卖家也可以通过海外经销商发布的行业资讯了解到最全面的行业全球走势,如主流销售国家的流行趋势、购物趋势、消费趋势等。

When registering an account, in addition to fill in the basic information of individual, users need to fill in detailed personal information, including education background, work experience and positions, language skills, etc. Then select to join groups or create groups, and establish contact with other users on LinkedIn. The home page of LinkedIn is shown in Figure 3-19.

注册账户时,除了填写个人基本信息,用户需要填写详细的个人简历信息,包括教育经历、工作经历及职务、掌握的语言等,选择想要参加的小组或建立群组,并和领英上其他用户建立联系。领英的首页如图3-19所示。

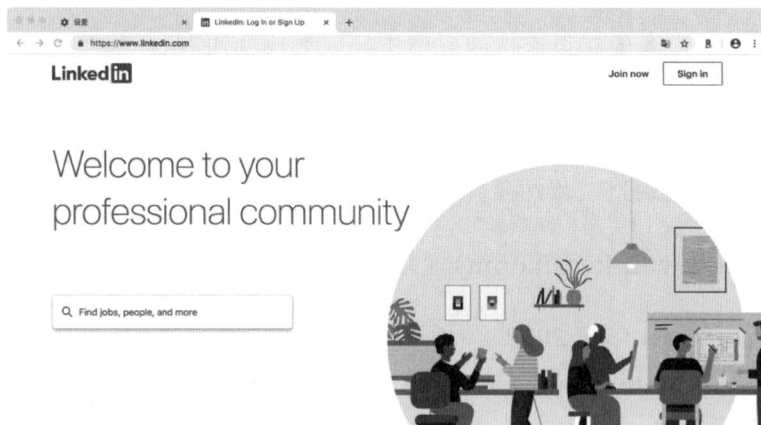

Figure 3-19 (图3-19)

There are some ways to manage LinkedIn account: ① Make full use of social relationships. In LinkedIn, free users can only add new contacts who are friends to existing friends, that is, users with common friends. In order to add contacts, sellers can also import contacts from other platforms to build their own business brand faster. ② Maintain activeness. For business-related discussions, interact with others effectively and share expertise to achieve high-quality traffic and increase brand awareness. ③ Make full use of LinkedIn advertising. The platform will push more users with subscription to sellers if they publish paid ads and thus help sellers to get targeted customers.

经营好领英账户有以下一些方法：①充分利用社会关系。在领英上，免费用户最多只能添加二度联系人，即有共同好友的用户。为了增加联系人，卖家也可以导入其他平台的联系人，从而更快建立起自己的业务品牌。②保持活跃度。针对开展的业务进行相关讨论，与他人进行有效互动，分享专业知识，从而获得高质量的流量和品牌知名度。③充分利用领英广告。发布付费广告将有助于推送订阅用户给卖家，可以帮助其获得目标客户。

# Section Four / **SEO**
## 搜索引擎优化

Search Engine Optimization (SEO) is a way to adjust the website to improve the ranking of the website in the search engine by understanding the operating rules of the search engine. SEO itself is free and can be used to attract traffic for websites 24 hours a day. The cost is mainly from labor.

搜索引擎优化，是一种通过了解搜索引擎的运作规则来调整网站，提高网站在搜索引擎内排名的方式。搜索引擎优化本身是免费的，能24小时为网站引流，其花费主要来自人力成本。

SEO is divided into the following three aspects: ①On-page SEO. It refers to the internal optimization of website, mainly for a series of related keywords to optimize the content of the page, including the optimization of the website code, URL, page description, etc. ② Off-page SEO. It refers to the external optimization of the website, mainly for the construction of external links. The more external links, the higher the link quality, and the higher the weighting of the website. ③ Technical SEO. It enables search engines to better capture and include the content.

搜索引擎优化分为以下三个方面：①站内优化。指网站内部优化，主要针对一系列有关联性的关键词来做网站页面内容的优化，包括网站的代码、URL、页面描述等的优化。②站外优化。指网站外部优化，主要针对外部链接的建设，外部链接做得越多，链接质量越高，网站的权重就会越高。③网站性能优化。它能让搜索引擎更好地抓取内容和收录内容。

According to research, for any search engine, 60% of users only look at the first three pages. Therefore, most websites want to improve the ranking in search engines in various ways. However, the search engine's algorithms are constantly updated, and the ranking of the website will change accordingly. Thus, search engine optimization is not once and for all. Users need to continue to work on SEO in order to maintain an ideal ranking.

根据研究显示,对于任何搜索引擎来说,60%的用户只看前三页的信息。因此,大部分的网站都希望通过各种方式来提升网站在搜索引擎中的排名。不过,搜索引擎的算法不断在更新,网站的排名也会因此变动,所以搜索引擎优化并非一劳永逸。用户需要持续做好搜索引擎优化,才能保持比较理想的排名。

Google's average monthly visits reached 47.7 billion, making it the most important search engine in the export cross-border e-commerce sector. In the website traffic source ranking, natural search is second only to direct search. In the Google search engine results page, as shown in Figure 3-20, Google ads occupy the upward position of four advertising space and downward position of three ones, the middle part is for the organic search results. For example, the traffic of Jollychic reached 10 million times in 3 months, of which 28.19% of the traffic comes from organic search; the traffic of Nike within 3 months reached 209 million times, of which 34.02% of the traffic comes from organic search.

谷歌平均每个月访问量达到477亿次,成为出口跨境电商领域最重要的搜索引擎。网站流量来源排名中,自然搜索占比仅次于直接搜索。在谷歌搜索引擎结果页面中,如图3-20所示,谷歌广告占据了"上四下三"的位置,中间部分为自然搜索结果。比如,执御在3个月内,平台访问量达到1000万次,其中28.19%的流量来自自然搜索;耐克在3个月内,平台访问量达到2.09亿次,其中34.02%的流量来自自然搜索。

As the world's largest technology company, Google is a search engine that serves hundreds of millions of Internet users. Google's primary concern is to help users find reliable and detailed information that users are looking for. If the editing way of the website is not standardized enough to match the preferences of Google search engine, that website won't get a good ranking. That's why it takes a lot of effort to optimize the site and optimize each page. The ultimate goal is to let Google know what your site is and what your page is talking about. For cross-border e-commerce practitioners, if you want to improve your product or store ranking in Google search engine, you can make efforts in the following aspects。

作为世界上最大的科技公司,谷歌的搜索引擎是服务于亿万网民的。第一时间让用

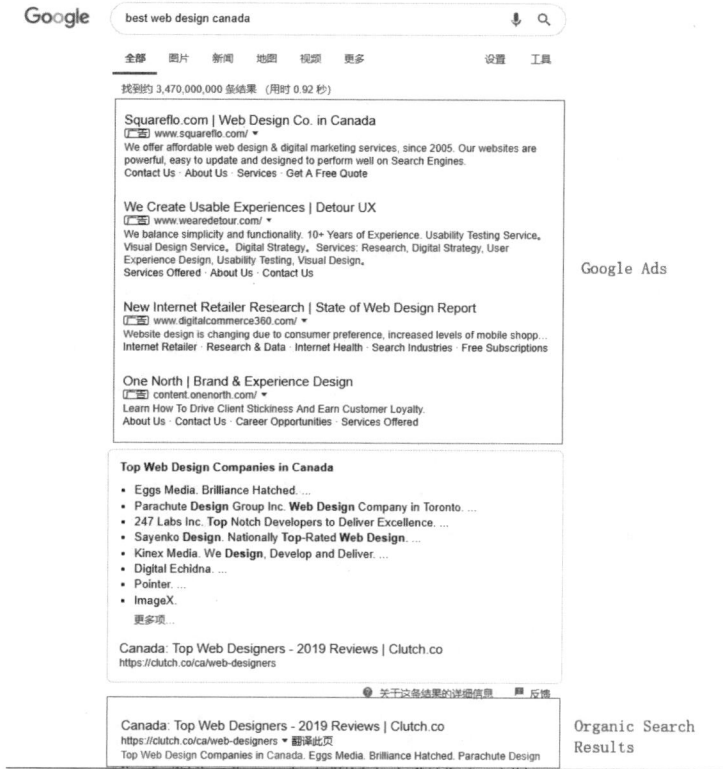

Figure 3-20（图 3-20）

户找到想要的、可靠的和详尽的信息是谷歌的首要关注点。如果网站编辑页面的方式不够规范,不符合谷歌搜索引擎的喜好,就不能获得好的排名。这就是为什么要花大力气去优化网站,优化每个页面,最终目的是让谷歌知道你的网站,知道你的页面在讲什么。对于跨境电商从业者来说,想要提升自己的产品或店铺在谷歌搜索引擎中的排名,可以从以下几个方面做出努力。

## 1. Decide the Direction for Optimization（制定优化方向）

Firstly, look at the problems of website code and structure through SEO audit tool. Secondly, sellers need to analyze the indicators including website visits (PV), number of keyword display and ranking, number of external links, and bounce rate to understand the status quo and problems of the website, so as to decide the optimization direction and goals of SEO.

首先,通过搜索引擎审计工具,卖家查看网站代码及结构上存在的问题。其次,卖家还要对包括网站访问量、关键词的展示量及排名、外链数,跳出率等指标进行分析,了解网站现状和问题,从而制定搜索引擎的方向和目标。

## 2. Improve Website Content (完善网站内容)

SEO is content-oriented, so optimizing the theme and content of the site are the most important. Only increasing clicking is not enough. Bounce rate and customer retention time are just as important. If the user leaves the site after 3 seconds, this is a bad user experience signal. Google will know that the user does not like your content. Therefore, it is necessary to write more high-quality content and increase attractive ways of introducing the content. By telling some vivid brand stories, customers can stay on website for a while and encourage them to share it with friends and bring sellers more potential buyers.

搜索引擎优化是以内容为主的,因而优化网站的主题和内容才是最重要的。仅有点击率是远远不够的,跳出率和客户留存时间也同样重要。如果用户在3秒后离开网站,这是一个不好的用户体验信号,谷歌会知道用户不喜欢你的内容。所以卖家要多写优质丰富的内容,增加吸引人的介绍方式。可以通过讲述一些生动的品牌故事,让客户在网站上多停留一会,并促使他们跟朋友进行分享,为卖家带来更多的潜在购买者。

It is not always good to have more content. The balance between quantity and quality should be maintained. When site has multiple pages showing the same product, the search engine will allow several of pages to compete with each other and sometimes even lower the ranking of the product. Combining these duplicates will prevent this from happening.

内容也并非越多越好,要保持数量和质量的平衡。当网站出现多个页面展示同一个产品时,搜索引擎会让网站的几个页面互相竞争,有时甚至会降低产品的排名。将这些重复的内容进行合并,就可以防止这种情况的出现。

## 3. Optimize Keywords (优化关键词)

The layout of keywords on the website is very important. It determines whether the website can be searched by users. Therefore, sellers should choose the most appropriate keywords and the right number of keywords according to the structure and importance of each page. The choice of keywords must be prominent and follow these principles: ① Keywords should be related to the topic of the website. Sellers should use the words related to the products and services the website needs to promote and will be most probably searched by users when using the search engine. ② Use different forms of the same keyword, including verb tenses and plurals, because search engines think they are completely unrelated (such as pet sitting, pet sitter, pet sitters, etc.). ③ Avoid using general vocabulary with a wide meaning and try to avoid jargon and abbreviations.

网站的关键词布局非常重要,它决定网站是否能被用户搜索到。因此卖家应根据每个页面的结构和页面的重要性,合理选择最合适的关键词和分配关键词个数。关键词的选择必须突出,遵循一定的原则,如:①关键词要与网站主题相关,选取人们在使用搜索引擎时常用到的与网站所需推广的产品及服务相关的词。②使用同一个关键词的不同变形,包括动词时态和复数,因为搜索引擎认为他们完全不相关(比如 pet sitting、pet sitter、pet sitters 等)。③避免使用含义很广的一般性词汇,尽量避免行话和缩略语。

Users can use the free third-party keyword search tool, such as Google AdWords or Word Tracker, to see how many times a keyword was searched in order to get inspired.

用户可以使用免费的第三方关键词搜索工具,例如 Google AdWords 或 Word Tracker,查看关键词被搜索的次数并获得灵感。

## 4. Build External Links (建设外部链接)

External links refer to links displayed on other websites that link to their own websites, which is a very important process for website optimization. The quality of the external link indirectly affects the weighting of website in the search engine. The effect of external links is not only to increase the weighting of website, but also to improve the ranking of a certain keyword. External link with high quality can bring good traffic to the site. After Google Penguin 4.0, if sellers buy a link or use an automated program to create a link, they will be punished by the search engine. A few years ago, the domestic foreign trade giant LightInTheBox and Milanoo network were identified as cheating by Google because of excessive SEO. Their websites were unable to display in the natural search results for a certain period of time.

外部链接指在其他网站导入自己网站的链接,对于网站优化来说是非常重要的一个过程。导入链接的质量间接影响网站在搜索引擎中的权重。建设外部链接不仅是为了提高网站的权重,也是为了提高某个关键词的排名。一个高质量的外部链接可以给网站带来很好的流量。Google Penguin 4.0 之后,如果卖家购买链接或使用自动程序创建链接,会受到搜索引擎的惩罚。前几年,国内的外贸巨头兰亭集势和米兰网都因为过度优化搜索引擎而被谷歌认定为作弊,其网站一度无法在自然搜索结果中显示。

## 5. Create a Better Mobile Experience (创造更好的移动体验)

In March 2018, Google announced its entry into the "Mobile Priority Index". Currently, more than half of cross-border e-commerce orders come from the mobile side, and this number is also rising. Users on the mobile side usually pay attention to a short period of time and have no patience to keep sliding down the page. In order to create a better mobile experience, sellers need to design a quick login page to make the menu as simple as possible, put contact information or contact buttons in a prominent position, as well as reduce the use of flashing fonts, plug-ins, pop-up pages and interstitial ads, etc. Sellers also need to take advantage of GPS positioning technology to optimize local search and pay attention to the different keywords that users search on PC and mobile end.

2018年3月,谷歌宣布进入"移动优先索引"。目前有超过一半的跨境电商订单来自移动端,这一数字也在不断上升。移动端的用户通常注意力集中的时间很短,也没有耐心一直下滑页面。为了创造更好的移动体验,卖家要设计快速登录页面,使菜单尽可能简单,将联系信息或联系按钮放在醒目的位置,减少使用闪烁字体、插件、弹出式页面和插页式广告等,利用GPS定位技术优化本地搜索,并且注意追踪用户在PC端和移动端搜索的不同关键词。

# Section Five / **Email Direct Marketing**
## 电子邮件营销

Email Direct Marketing (EDM) refers to an online marketing method that delivers valuable information to target users through emails with the prior permission of users. Through regular emails, the purpose is to enable businesses and consumers to establish contact and promote sales.

电子邮件营销,简称EDM,是指在用户事先许可的前提下,通过电子邮件的方式向目标用户传递有价值信息的一种网络营销手段。通过定期的邮件,其目的在于让企业和消费者建立起联系,达到促进销售的目的。

Many European and American consumers have the habit of frequently checking emails. Email is an important way for them to contact others and receive outside news. Therefore, EDM is also crucial for sellers in the European and American markets. And EDM has the characteristics of low cost, simpleness, accurate positioning, informative contents, fast speed and effective marketing. It is the second highest ROI marketing channel, ranking only second to SNS.

很多欧美消费者有频繁查收邮件的习惯,邮件是他们联系他人、接收外界消息的重要途径。因此,对于开辟欧美市场的卖家来说,电子邮件营销也至关重要。并且电子邮件营销具有成本低、简单直接、定位精准、内容丰富、传播速度快、营销效果明显等特点,是投资回报率第二高的一种营销渠道,仅次于社交媒体营销。

EDM needs to pay attention to the following aspects: ① Before creating a user database, cross-border e-commerce sellers must get the consumer's authorization of sending product promotion advertisements. The authorization can generally be completed through website registration or membership information systems. From the anti-spam laws of various countries, unauthorized advertising mails are generally characterized as spam. ② Produce high-quality and attractive emails in terms of title, content, layout, colors, etc. The title of the message often determines whether consumers will open the message, so a compelling title is critical. In terms of content, foreign customers are very interested in some traditional Chinese culture and traditional elements. Sellers can combine the Chinese traditional elements, local manners and consumption habits with the products as much as possible, as well as try to avoid some taboos. ③ Use the user information collected in the previous period for accurate mail delivery.

电子邮件营销需要注意以下几个环节:①创建用户数据库前,跨境电商卖家必须经过消费者的许可,才能把商品促销广告发送到消费者的邮箱中。这种许可一般可以通过网站注册或者会员信息制度等完成。从各国的反垃圾邮件法来看,未经许可的广告邮件一般都会被定性为垃圾邮件。②制作优质的、有吸引力的邮件内容,包括邮件标题、内容设置、布局排版、颜色搭配等。邮件的标题一般决定着消费者是否打开邮件,因此需要创建一个引人注目的标题。在内容设置方面,国外的客户对中国的一些传统文化和传统元素都是非常感兴趣的,卖家可以从这方面入手,并尽可能地结合自己的商品进行专业的文案制作,同时结合客户的地区风俗习惯和消费习惯,尽量规避一些禁忌。③利用前期收集到的用户信息进行精准的邮件投放。

EDM includes personalized promotional mails and exclusive discounts to encourage regular customers to purchase continuously, holiday greetings and new & hot product recommendations to attract new and existing customers to pay special attention to the brand. Here are a few examples of brands.

电子邮件营销方式包括用个性化的促销邮件、独家的折扣来鼓励老客户连续购买,用假日主题的问候、新品爆品推荐等方式来吸引新老客户持续关注品牌。以下选取了几个品牌的案例。

## 1. Holiday Discount（节假日折扣）

Traditional American holidays include New Year, Valentine's Day, Easter, Halloween, Thanksgiving Day and Christmas. During these holidays, consumption and expenses will rise sharply. Therefore, as a cross-border e-commerce seller, you must not miss the business opportunities of holidays.

美国传统的节假日有新年、情人节、复活节、万圣节、感恩节和圣诞节等，在这些节假日期间，消费支出会大幅上升，因此作为跨境电商卖家，必然不能错过节假日的商机。

As shown in Figure 3-21, it is a promotional picture of Black Friday of Walmart. It displays the information on tech deals, toys deals, sports deals, fashion deals and home deals. Black Friday is the time for all Americans to buy discounted products. Merchants will also issue coupons or post discount information to attract customers in advance. In the US, the first Monday after Thanksgiving Day is Cyber Monday. It is also the biggest online shopping day of the year. Compared to Black Friday, which the day for buying electronic products, Cyber Monday is the day for buying makeups, shoes and booking hotels.

图3-21是沃尔玛"黑色星期五"促销的邮件图片，分类展示了电子产品、玩具、体育用品、时尚产品、家居产品等折扣信息。黑色星期五，是美国全民打折购物的时间，商家也会提前通过电子邮件发放优惠券或刊登打折信息来吸引顾客。美国还有"剁手星期一"，是感恩节之后的第一个星期一，是一年中最大的网络购物日。相比在"黑色星期五"适合买电子产品，在"剁手星期一"更适合买美妆产品、鞋子，以及预订酒店等。

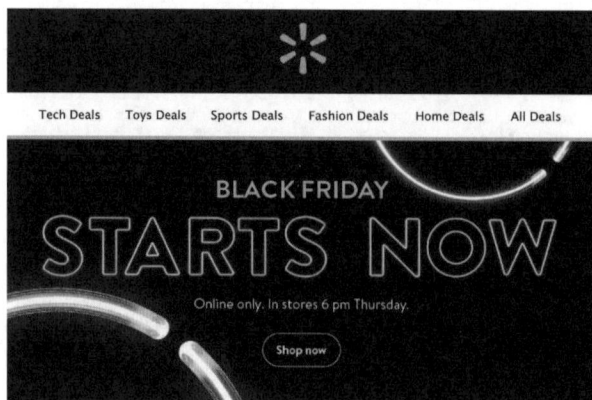

Figure 3-21（图3-21）

## 2. Mid-Season Promotions (季中促销活动)

Online discount offers are a win-win strategy for both retailers and customers. For any e-commerce marketer, it's nothing new to incorporate discounts into their strategy. Since 55% of customers prefer to cut prices instead of loyalty rewards or free shipping, the announcement of mid-season promotions will undoubtedly increase online sales.

在线折扣优惠对零售商和客户是一个双赢的策略。对于任何电商营销人员来说,将折扣纳入他们的策略并不是什么新鲜的事情。由于55%的客户更希望降价,而不是忠诚奖励或免费送货,因此宣布季中促销活动无疑能够提升电商销量。

Figure 3-22 shows the summer season promotion mail from Anthropologie. The design of this picture is fresh, beautiful and elegant. It also shows the discount, which will not make customers feel resentful. And it conveys clear brand information, which drives brand advocates to take faster action.

图3-22所示的是来自Anthropologie的夏日季中促销邮件,设计美观大方,并说明了折扣情况,不会让顾客产生反感的情绪。并且它传达了清晰的品牌信息,能够促使品牌拥护者更快地采取行动。

**EXTRA 30% OFF TAG SALE**
shop just-added styles

**ANTHROPOLOGIE**

**25% OFF**
*summer essentials*

SHOP THE EDIT →

Figure 3-22 (图3-22)

## 3. Birthday Discount (生日折扣)

Customers always expect to be valued and get special treatment from the brand. So when merchants use personalized emails to tell regular customers that they understand them and remember their details, brand trust and loyalty can be gained.

客户总是希望自己能够得到重视,得到品牌的特殊待遇。因此当商家使用个性化邮件向老客户表达自己了解他们,并记住他们的细节时,可以建立品牌信任和忠诚度。

To celebrate the customer's birthday, Blue Nile will send an email to the customer (shown in Figure 3-23) and offer special offers to help customers save money on buying products. Once customers receive the email, they will feel special and be encouraged to visit the website to learn more about the related products. For a brand, this is a good way to build brand loyalty and drive sales.

为了纪念客户的生日,Blue Nile会发送一封邮件祝福客户(见图3-23),并提供特别优惠,帮助客户节省购买品牌产品的费用。一旦客户收到这封邮件,他们就会觉得自己很特别,并且会受到鼓励进入网站来了解更多相关产品的信息。对于一个品牌来说,这是建立品牌忠诚度和推动电商销售的好方法。

Figure 3-23 (图 3-23)

## 4. Flash Sales (限时抢购活动)

Flash Sales refers to a relatively low price for exclusive members to purchase within a specified time. It is usually first come first served, with limited time and quantity. This mode originated in France and was later introduced by other countries. As shown in Figure 3-24, it's the mail notification of Victoria's Secret Flash Sales. An exclusive discount code is usually provided in the email by merchants.

　　限时抢购活动指以比较低的折扣供专属会员在指定的时间内购得，先到先得，限时限量，售完即止。该模式起源于法国，后被其他国家效仿。图3-24所示的是维多利亚的秘密限时抢购活动的邮件通知，一般在邮件中会提供专属的折扣码。

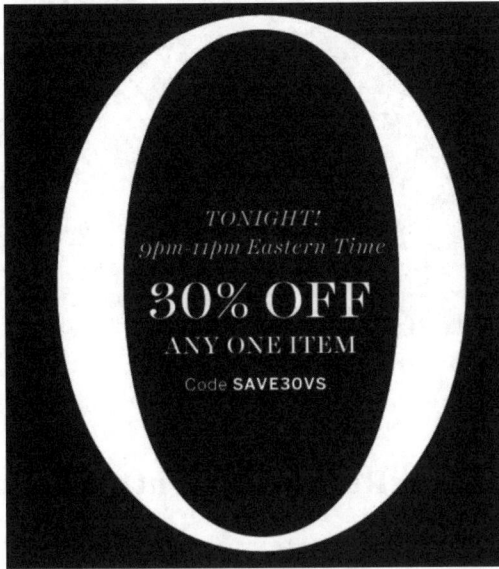

Figure 3-24 (图3-24)

## 5. Newly Released & Bestsellers（新品及畅销产品速递）

Merchants can also regularly send a summary list of newly released and bestsellers to cater to consumer demand for seasonal merchandise. It can increase brand familiarity and sales of new and best-selling items. Figure 3-25 is a new product recommendation email from Massimo Dutti, which contains 3 to 5 other products and has website links. The style of the brand is simple, and it is consistent with the style of the email. It is not only based on casual and professional design concepts, but also captures the latest fashion elements.

　　商家还可以定期发送新品和畅销产品的汇总列表，迎合消费者储备季节性商品的需求，提升品牌熟悉度，以及新品和畅销单品的销量。图3-25是 Massimo Dutti 的新品推荐邮件，该邮件内含有其他3—5款产品，并且设有官网链接。该品牌风格简洁，在基于随意及职业性的设计理念的同时，捕捉最新的时尚元素，和邮件风格一致。

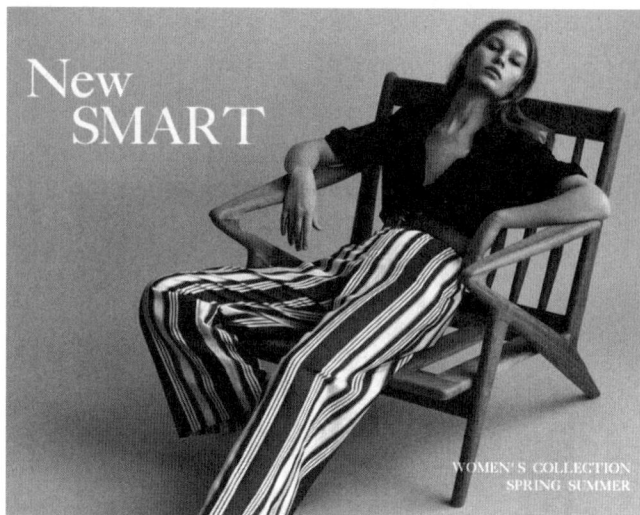

Figure 3-25 (图 3-25)

## Section Six / **Extensive Reading: LightInTheBox**
拓展阅读：兰亭集势

LightInTheBox is an online B2C cross-border e-commerce company that integrates supply chain services. It operates on its own e-commerce platform, as well as opening store on overseas e-commerce platforms such as Amazon and eBay, to sell high-quality products to customers around the world at reasonable prices. LightInTheBox integrates e-commerce and overseas social media marketing to fully consider the characteristics of different social marketing platforms, and brings different effects of perception to users in various forms with low cost, thus gradually attracting users' attention and interest, improving product awareness, as well as spreading brand image. The logo is shown in Figure 3-26.

兰亭集势是整合供应链生态圈服务的在线 B2C 跨境电商公司。它通过自有的电商平台，以及在亚马逊和易贝等海外电商平台上开店的方式，旨在以亲民的价格，将优质的商品带给全球客户。兰亭集势将电商与海外社交营销媒体相结合，充分考虑不同社交营销平台的特点，以丰富的形式和较低的成本带给用户不同的感知效果，从而逐渐凝聚用户的关注与兴趣，拓展产品认知度，传播品牌形象。图 3-26 是兰亭集势的标志。

# Light in thebox.com

Figure 3-26 (图 3-26)

LightInTheBox has registered social accounts on Facebook, Twitter, Pinterest, You Tube and Instagram. Take Facebook as an example, the number of daily posting of LightInTheBox is around 4-5, and the time interval between postings is about 4 hours. It avoids the feeling of brushing the screen for fans and will help to increase traffic. What is more important is the content of every post. LightInTheBox's Facebook postings mainly include the following six categories: creative posts, fashion posts, funny posts, festival posts, customer photo posts and other posts.

兰亭集势在 Facebook、Twitter、Pinterest、You Tube 和 Instagram 等平台上都注册了社交账户。以脸书为例,兰亭集势的日均发帖数量保持在 4—5 个,每次发帖的时间间隔在 4 小时左右,避免给粉丝带来刷屏的感觉,有助于引流。更重要的是帖子内容,兰亭集势脸书的发帖主要有以下六大类:创意新奇帖、潮流时尚帖、幽默有趣帖、节庆活动帖、顾客晒图帖和其他帖。

The most popular ones are fashion posts, which evoke the desire of fans to purchase after seeing beautiful and fashionable images and attractive descriptions. LightInTheBox also can have good interactions with fans by raising questions. LightInTheBox focuses on clothes. Through fashion posts, it not only highlights the style of the website, but also maximizes traffic and conversion rates. The second influential posts are creative posts. Everyone loves creative products, so it's easy to get fans'likes, comments, and forward. Of course, more importantly, young fans will be much happier to click on the link to find more similar products and place an order. Next one is the festival posts. For example, near Halloween, the official website can send out a few interesting holiday dress-up photos to attract fans to the site to buy related products. In addition, LightInTheBox will also engage in activities such as Give Away Time and Flash Sale from time to time to attract fans. Finally, funny posts make the official commercial website more interesting. The pictures and user experience posted by customers after receiving their products are regarded as word-of-mouth marketing, and it is also the most convincing marketing method. For example, LightInTheBox will publish the pictures and comments that are posted by customers, and give customers the most sincere praise and gratitude. All fans can see it and this practice will attract more fans to place orders. In addition, LightInTheBox will also send positive posts, landscape photos, interactive posts, etc., so that fans feel that they are interacting with a real person, not a commercial enterprise.

其中最多的是潮流时尚帖，精美时尚的产品图片和地道的说明性语言可唤起粉丝的购买欲。配上提问，可与粉丝良好互动。兰亭集势主打服饰类产品，通过潮流时尚帖不仅可以彰显网站风格，而且能最大限度引入流量，并获取转化率。数量第二多的是创意新奇帖。每个人都喜欢有创意的新奇类产品，因此这类帖子很容易得到粉丝的赞、评论以及转发。当然，更重要的是，年轻粉丝们会非常乐意点击链接发现更多类似产品，并下单购买。接下来是节庆活动帖。例如，临近万圣节，官网可以发出几张有趣的节日装扮照片，吸引粉丝进入网站购买相关产品。此外，兰亭集势还会时不时举办一些礼券赠送、限时闪购等活动，吸引粉丝参与。最后，幽默有趣帖让带有商业性质的官网主页变得更加可爱，也能起到吸引关注的作用。顾客购买产品之后晒出的图片和使用心得属于口碑营销，也是最具有说服力的营销手段。例如，兰亭集势会把顾客晒出的图片和评语都公布出来，并给予顾客最真诚的赞美和感谢，可以让所有粉丝看到，吸引更多粉丝下单。此外，兰亭集势还会布发正能量帖子、风景照帖子、话题互动性帖子等，让粉丝感觉是在跟一个真实的人互动，而不是一家商业化的企业。

In addition to posts, social media operators may also need to process customers' complaints. In the face of customer complaints, operators must respond carefully to show that they pay great attention to consumers. And it is best to guide customers to send private messages, so as not to deal with disputes in front of millions of fans, which will undermine the brand image.

除了发帖，社交媒体的运营人员还可能需要处理顾客的投诉留言。面对顾客的投诉性留言，运营人员一定要认真回复，以表示对消费者的重视。同时最好引导顾客发私信，以免在千万粉丝面前处理纠纷破坏品牌形象。

In addition to running the official company page, enterprises can also apply for other accounts to form a subsidiary page that specializes in specific topics (such as fashion & luxury, etc.) to attract specific people to join. Moreover, paying for Facebook ads or working with online celebrities can also be very effective, but enterprises also need to consider the input-output ratio of marketing and budget before choosing a paid marketing channel.

除了运营好企业官方专页，企业还可以申请其他账号，形成附属专页，专门运营某个特定主题（比如时尚奢侈品等），以吸引特定人群加入。另外，付费购买脸书广告或者与网络红人合作，也能起到很好的营销效果，但企业在选择付费营销途径前也需要考虑营销预算和投入产出比。

Adapted from www.cifnews.com （改编自雨果网）

# Chapter Four
## Cross-Border Logistics

# 跨境电商物流

## Lead-in

## 导入

With the rapid development of cross-border e-commerce in China, the number of cross-border parcels continues to grow rapidly, which also promotes the development of cross-border logistics industry. As an important component of cross-border e-commerce, cross-border logistics affects the purchasing experience and satisfaction of consumers. How to choose cross-border logistics with low freight rate, fast speed and strong customs clearance ability is key in gaining competitive advantage for sellers. This chapter will introduce the concept, characteristics, main modes and selection criteria of cross-border logistics.

随着我国跨境电商的迅速发展,跨境包裹数量持续快速增长,也推动了跨境物流行业的发展。跨境物流作为跨境电商的重要环节,影响着消费者的购买体验和满意度。如何选择运费价格低、速度快、通关能力强的跨境物流是卖家能否在竞争中取得优势的关键点。本章会依次介绍跨境物流的概念、特征、主要模式和选择依据等内容。

## Section One / **Overview of Cross-Border Logistics**

## 跨境物流概述

Cross-border logistics refers to transportation and distribution services between different countries or regions. Cross-border logistics is a form that shows the development of logistics services to an advanced stage. Since the two parties of cross-border e-commerce belong to different countries or regions, the goods need to be transferred from the supplier country or region by way of cross-border logistics to the country or region where the buyer is located, as well as distributing and delivering the products. Compared with domestic logistics, cross-border logistics needs to be distributed all over the world, involving customs of importing and exporting countries, as well as customs clearance and commodity inspection. It is also linked with laws, politics, economics, cultural, language and other factors of different countries or regions. Thus the work is more complicated. Few enterprises can independently handle and complete this part of business only relying on their own resources.

跨境物流指在不同国家或地区之间进行的运输配送服务,是物流服务发展到高级阶段的一种表现形式。由于跨境电子商务的交易双方分属不同国家或地区,商品需要从供应方国家或地区通过跨境物流方式实现空间位置转移,在买方所在的国家或地区内实现最后的物流与配送。与境内物流相比,跨境物流需要跨越国界,在全世界范围内进行配送,涉及进口国海关和出口国海关,需要进行清关与商检,还与各个国家或地区的法律、政治、经济、文化、语言等因素联系,工作内容较复杂,很少有企业可以依靠自身能力单独办理并完成这部分业务。

Cross-border e-commerce logistics belongs to the service industry. The emerging logistics information industry, logistics technology equipment manufacturing industry and logistics finance industry all restrict the formation and development of cross-border e-commerce logistics competitiveness in China. In recent years, logistics finance has also developed rapidly in China. At present, almost all banks have already carried out logistics finance business, but there are still many shortcomings, including lack of perfect credit system, low service efficiency, complicated procedures, and slow capital turnover.

跨境电商物流属于第三服务产业,新兴的物流信息产业、物流技术装备制造业和物流金融产业都制约着我国跨境电商业物流竞争力的形成与提升。近几年,物流金融在我国也得到了快速的发展。目前,几乎所有的银行都已开展了物流金融业务,但是还存在着诸多的不足,包括信用体系不完善、服务效率低、手续复杂、资金周转慢等。

With the rapid development of cross-border e-commerce, China has become an important battleground for the competition of major express companies around the world. The postal network is basically covered all over the world, and it is wider than any other logistics with relatively low price. However, these parcels generally leave the country privately and are unable to enjoy the normal export tax return. Moreover, the speed is slow and the parcel loss rate is relatively high. Several domestic private express companies, including SF Express, Deppon Express, five major express companies (YTO Express, STO Express, ZTO Express, Best Express and Yunda) provide logistics services for cross-border e-commerce enterprises through self-built branches or local partners. International express delivery giants including DHL, FedEx, TNT and UPS have strong economic strength, supported by global self-built networks and international information systems. They can use advanced express sorting system and information inquiry system to provide various value-added services and personalized services. Compared with China's newly-started cross-border e-commerce logistics enterprises, international express delivery giants have developed for many years and have won certain market recognition through high-quality service. At the same time, the cross-border e-commerce platforms have also launched special line logistics services. For example, AliExpress online delivery services provide Russian special logistics such as Speed Express, Russian Express and other Russian special line logistics, and provide Yanwen special line logistics and for 22 countries including Russia, Brazil and Indonesia, etc. In recent years, the successive opening of international railways such as "YIXINOU China–Europe Railway" and "YUXINOU China–Europe Railway" and the gradual improvement of logistics infrastructure along the route also contributes to the development of cross-border e-commerce logistics along "the Belt and Road" region.

随着跨境电商的迅猛发展,我国成了全球各大快递公司竞争的重要战场。邮政快递的网络基本覆盖全球,比其他任何物流渠道都要广,价格也非常便宜。但是这种包裹一般以私人包裹方式出境,无法享受正常的出口退税,而且速度较慢,丢包率高。国内几大民营快递公司,包括顺丰快递、德邦快递、"四通一达(圆通、申通、中通、汇通和韵达)"通过自建网点或寻找当地合作伙伴,为跨境电商企业提供物流服务。敦豪快递、联邦快递、天地快递、联合包裹等国际快递巨头具有雄厚的经济实力,以全球自建网络以及国际化信息系统为支撑,运用当今最先进的快递分拣系统和信息查询系统,能够提供各种增值服务和个性化的服务。对比我国刚起步的跨境电商物流企业,国际快递巨头已经发展了很多年,并且以高质量的服务水平赢得了一定的市场认可度。同时,跨境电商平台也推出了专线物流服务,比如速卖通线上发货服务提供了速优宝、俄速通等俄罗斯专线物流,针对俄罗斯、巴西、印尼等22个国家提供燕文专线等。近年来,"义新欧中欧铁路"和"渝新欧中欧铁路"等国际铁路的相继开通和沿线物流基础设施的逐步完善也有助于"一带一路"沿线地区跨境电商物流的发展。

During the period of 2011—2016 when cross-border e-commerce is becoming increasingly mature, China's cross-border e-commerce express business has maintained a rapid growth trend, with a growth rate of 61.5% in 2013, 44.6% and 28% in 2016 and 2017 respectively. The growth rate has gradually slowed down. In 2017, China's cross-border e-commerce consumer complaints accounted for 12.98% of the total number of complaints, of which logistics-related complaints accounted for 21%. The drawbacks of cross-border e-commerce logistics are obvious, including long delivery time, high logistics costs, customs clearance barriers, after-sales problems and the lack of specialized third-party logistics services. These problems have restricted the development of cross-border e-commerce in China to some extent.

在跨境电子商务日趋成熟的2011—2016年,我国跨境电商快递业业务量保持着高速增长的趋势,2013年增速高达61.5%,2016年和2017年分别为44.6%和28%,增速逐步放缓。2017年我国跨境电商消费者投诉占投诉总量的12.98%,其中与物流有关的投诉占比达21%,跨境电商物流短板凸显,存在配送时间长、物流成本高、清关障碍、售后困难,以及缺少专业化的第三方物流服务等问题,在一定程度上制约了我国跨境电商的发展。

(1) Long delivery time. The delivery time of cross-border e-commerce logistics is far longer than that of domestic e-commerce. For example, the delivery time of international e-packet to the main regions of Europe and America is around ten days to half a month, and it takes at least forty to fifty days to arrive in Russia and other places. These weeks and even months of delivery time are sometimes beyond the patience of overseas consumers, reduce the shopping experience, and seriously hinder the development of cross-border e-commerce.

配送时间长。跨境电商物流的配送时间远远比境内电商的长。比如,国际e邮宝到欧美主要地区的时间为十天到十五天,到达俄罗斯等地至少需四五十天。这些长达几周甚至几月的配送时间,考验着海外消费者的耐心,降低了购物体验,也严重阻碍了跨境电商的发展。

(2) High logistics costs. Logistics costs include transportation and warehousing, which typically account for 30% of total costs, and logistics costs for cross-border e-commerce in China are higher. In the case of DHL, the cost of 500g goods shipped from China to Japan is around RMB100, and extra customs duties, additional fees and fuel surcharges are required. If you add the logistics cost of return and exchange, the cost of cross-border e-commerce logistics will be more than three times the normal logistics cost. Thus, sometimes the profit of an order is not enough to pay the express fee. If the seller adds the logistics cost to commodity price, the price advantage of cross-border e-commerce product compared to overseas local product will be greatly weakened.

物流成本高。物流成本包括运输和仓储,一般占总成本的三成,中国跨境电商的物流成本则更高。以中外运敦豪为例,500克重的商品从中国运到日本,需要100元左右的快递费,并且需另收关税、附加费和燃油附加费。如果再加上退换货的物流费用,跨境电商物流成本将是正常物流成本的3倍以上,以至于经常出现一笔订单的利润还不够支付快递费用的现象。如果卖家将物流成本分摊到商品价格中，那么跨境电商产品与海外本土产品的价格优势也被极大地削弱了。

(3) Customs clearance barriers. Cross-border e-commerce goods need to pass the customs of the exporting country and the customs of the destination country respectively. According to the customs policy of each country, it is necessary to go through multiple declaration procedures and it will generate expenses. It may also encounter customs inspections in the importing country, face the problem of direct confiscation, return of goods or replenishing customs declaration materials. The complicated customs clearance process also prolongs the delivery time of logistics and restricts the development of cross-border e-commerce.

清关障碍。跨境电商货物在运输过程中，需要通过出口国海关和目的国海关两道关卡。根据各国海关的政策，需要经过多层的申报手续并由此产生许多费用，还可能会遇到进口国海关扣货查验，面临直接没收、退回货物或再补充报关材料的处理结果。烦琐的通关过程同时延长了物流的运送时间，制约着跨境电商的发展。

(4) Problems in after-sales services. For cross-border e-commerce consumers, the problems of return and exchange due to unmatched items, size problems, damage during logistics are inevitable. Moreover, in developed countries of Europe and North America, consumers can return their products within a certain period of time without any reason. However, product return is a difficult problem due to long-term cross-border logistics, high cost, difficult customs clearance, etc. If you encounter a quality problem or need after-sales services for home appliances, the seller may need to spend a higher cost to set up a local after-sales team or directly return the full amount to the buyer.

售后困难。对于跨境电商消费者而言，由于货不对板、尺码问题、物流过程中的破损等导致的退换货问题是不可避免的。而且，在欧美地区的发达国家存在着无理由退货的消费习惯和文化。但是由于跨境物流存在时间长、成本高、通关难等问题，跨境电商退换货是个难题。如果碰到有质量问题或需要售后的家电产品，卖家就需要花费较高费用组建当地的售后团队或直接把全款退给买家。

(5) Lack of specialized third-party logistics services. Due to the rapid development of cross-border e-commerce in China, the logistics timeliness, distribution equipment and distribution services of traditional domestic enterprises are difficult to meet the development of cross-border e-commerce. The high-end logistics services and value-added services are lacking, as well as a series of other services such as logistics

system integration, supply chain optimize solutions, big data logistics, and cloud computing information platforms. Specialized third-party logistics services, efficient and reasonable logistics systems and complete logistics facilities are necessary to promote the sustainable development of cross-border e-commerce in China and increase the market competitiveness of our products.

缺少专业化的第三方物流服务。由于我国跨境电商发展迅速，境内传统企业的物流时效、配送设备、配送服务等都难以满足跨境电商的发展，物流高端服务与增值服务缺失，无法提供物流系统集成、供应链优化解决方案、大数据物流、云计算信息平台等一系列服务。专业化的第三方物流服务、高效合理的物流体系和完备的物流设施对推动我国跨境电子商务可持续发展、增强我国产品的市场竞争力是非常有必要的。

# Section Two / **Main Modes of Cross-Border Logistics**
## 跨境物流主要模式

## 1. Postal Parcel Mode (邮政包裹模式)

China Post is a member of the Universal Postal Union (UPU) and Kahala Post Cooperation Organization (KPG). It covers the whole world and has an absolute advantage in price over international express. As shown in Figure 4-1, the UPU is an intergovernmental international organization that negotiates international postal services. Its predecessor was Postal General Union, which was established on October 9, 1874. Since July 1, 1978, the UPU has become a specialized agency of the United Nations on international postal services. Headquartered in Bern, the capital of Switzerland, the UPU aims to promote, organize and improve international postal services, develop international cooperation in postal services, as well as provide postal technical assistance to member countries. However, due to the large number of UPU member countries, the level of postal development between member countries is different, and it is difficult to promote deep postal cooperation between member countries. As a result, the postal departments of China, Japan, South Korea, the United States, etc., held postal CEO summits in Kahala Oriental Hotel, Hawaii, in 2002, and formed the KPG. And later, France, Singapore, Spain and Britain also joined the organization. The organization has strict requirements on the delivery timeliness of all member countries. If the goods are not delivered within the specified time, the operator is responsible for delivery needs to return the postage. These strict requirements have prompted deepening cooperation among member countries and improved service levels.

中国邮政是万国邮政联盟和卡哈拉邮政合作组织的成员，网点基本覆盖全球，在价格上相对国际快递有绝对优势。如图4-1所示，万国邮政联盟，简称"万国邮联"，是商定国际邮政事务的政府间国际组织，其前身是1874年10月9日成立的邮政总联盟。万国邮联自1978年7月1日起成为联合国关于国际邮政事务的专门机构，总部设在瑞士首都伯尔尼，宗旨是促进、组织和改善国际邮政业务，发展邮政方面的国际合作，并在力所能及的范围内给予会员国所要求的邮政技术援助。但由于万国邮联会员国众多，会员国之间的邮政发展水平不一，很难促成会员国之间的深度邮政合作。于是，中国、日本、韩国、美国等国家和地区的邮政部门于2002年在美国夏威夷卡哈拉东方饭店召开了邮政CEO高峰会议，会后组成了卡哈拉邮政合作组织，后来，法国、新加坡、西班牙和英国也加入了该组织。该组织对所有成员国的投递时效有严格的要求，如果货物在指定时间内未送达，负责投递的运营商需要退赔邮资。这些严格的要求都促使会员国之间深化合作，提升服务水平。

Figure 4-1（图4-1）

According to incomplete statistics, about 70% of China's cross-border e-commerce export business is sent to overseas through postal parcels, of which China Post accounts for about 50%. China Post's services mainly include Postal Parcel, e-Packet, e-Express, e-Speed and so on. Chinese sellers will also use other postal services including Hongkong Post and Singapore Post.

据不完全统计，中国出口跨境电商业务中约有70%的包裹通过邮政包裹发送到海外，其中中国邮政约占50%的份额。中国邮政的服务主要包括邮政小包、e邮宝、e特快和e速宝等。中国卖家还会使用其他邮政，如中国香港邮政、新加坡邮政等。

The Postal Parcel is an economical international express service, which is widely used by sellers because of its advantages of low price, good timeliness, convenient customs clearance and wide delivery range. The Postal Parcel is divided into China Post registered air mail and post ordinary air mail, both of which have more restrictions on the volume, weight and shape of the merchandise. China Post registered air mail has registration fee, and the logistics details can be inquired through the official website of China Post. China Post ordinary air mail is a more economical package. There is no registration service, and the tracking information cannot be inquired. The security and stability are not as good as China Post registered air mail. Therefore, there is a certain limit on the AliExpress platform for the seller to use China Post ordinary air mail. For example, if the actual payment of the parcel is greater than 5 dollars and it is sent to the United States, sellers cannot use China Post ordinary air mail.

邮政小包是一项经济实惠的国际快件服务项目,因价格便宜、时效尚可、清关方便、派送范围广等优势而被卖家广泛使用。邮政小包分为邮政挂号小包和邮政平常小包,两者在商品的体积、重量、形状等方面都有较多限制。邮政挂号小包需要支付挂号费,物流详情可以通过中国邮政官网进行查询。邮政平常小包则是一款更为经济的小包,没有挂号服务,无法查询跟踪信息,安全性和稳定性较差。因此,在速卖通平台对卖家使用邮政平常小包发货有一定限制。比如,寄往美国的包裹如果实际支付金额大于5美元就不可以使用邮政平常小包。

e-Packet is an economical international postal service created by China Post for cross-border e-commerce in China. It is an airmail service for light and small items. Currently, the business is limited to providing delivery services for Chinese e-commerce sellers to countries including the United States, Canada, Britain, France and Australia. The delivery time is fast. For example, it only takes 7–12 days for international e-Packet on eBay to deliver products within the United States, and the price is also affordable.

e邮宝是中国邮政为中国跨境电商卖打造的一款经济型国际邮递产品,针对轻小件物品的空邮产品。目前,该业务仅限于为中国电商卖家提供发向美国、加拿大、英国、法国和澳大利亚的包裹寄递服务。e邮宝时效快,比如易贝上的国际e邮宝美国全境妥投时间甚至能达到7—12天,价格也比较实惠。

e-Express is a high-end cross-border e-commerce logistics service developed by China Post. It has covered 15 countries and regions and has a weight limit of 30 kg. The customs clearance ability of e-Express is strong. e-Express has the priority of processing services in different countries' customs, and it is flexible in counting products. The light and small characteristics are in line with the characteristics of cross-border e-commerce sales products. Like e-Packet, you can directly connect the information to the cross-border e-commerce system. Customers can print detailed information online, submit information for pick-up services, or send the products in person.

e特快是中国邮政开发的一款高端跨境电商物流产品,目前已通达15个国家和地区,限重30千克。e特快通关能力强,可享受各国海关优先处理服务,计重灵活,符合跨境电商销售产品轻、小的特征。和e邮宝一样,e特快也可以直接与跨境电商系统对接,客户在线打印详情单,提交揽收信息,或上门自送。

e-Package is an economical express delivery service designed by China Post logistics to meet the needs of cross-border e-commerce products and overseas postal services. It serves the seller of e-commerce platforms that send bulk items. The product is limited to 30 kg, and the time limit is 5-7 working days.

e包裹是邮政速递物流为适应跨境电商重件产品市场需求与境外邮政联合设计开办的经济型速递产品,服务于寄送批量物品的电商平台卖家,产品限重30千克,时限参考为5—7个工作日。

e-Speed is a commercial logistics solution for cross-border e-commerce sellers with light products developed by China Post. It must declare the details of the goods, the tariff number, the declared value and the weight. The time limit is 7-10 working days and the cost is relatively lower.

e速宝是中国邮政针对轻小件跨境电商卖家的商业渠道物流解决方案,须详细申报物品明细、税则号、申报价值和重量。时限参考为7—10个工作日,资费较低。

China Hongkong Post Air Mail refers to the international packet sent by China Hongkong Post to foreign customers. At present, most of the mainland eBay sellers choose to ship through China Hongkong Post and the products need to transfer to Hong Kong, which is different from the postal delivery in the Mainland.

中国香港邮政小包,是指通过香港邮政发送到国外客户手中的国际小包。目前中国内地的易贝卖家大多选择通过香港邮政发货,货物需要转运到香港,其和内地的邮政发货不一样。

Singapore Post Packet, also known as the Singapore Post Air Parcel and Singapore Registered Parcel, is a postal parcel service launched by Singapore Post for goods weighing less than 2 kg. Compared with China Post and China Hongkong Post, the biggest advantage is that customers can send products with electricity. For the Southeast Asian market, the services, timeliness and charges of Singapore Post are also advantageous.

新加坡邮政小包,即新加坡邮政航空小包裹,又叫新加坡挂号小包,是新加坡邮政推出的一项针对货物重量在2千克以下的邮政小包服务。与中国邮政小包和中国香港邮政小包相比,其最大的优势是可以寄带电产品。对于东南亚市场,新加坡邮政的服务、时效及收费也颇具优势。

## 2. International Express Mode (国际快递模式)

Another logistics mode commonly used by cross-border e-commerce sellers is international express delivery. The four major international express giants were DHL, UPS, FedEx and TNT. In 2017, after FedEx completed the acquisition of the old Dutch company TNT, the four major international express giants officially became the top three, and the concentration was further strengthened. International express mode has the advantages of timeliness and low packet loss rate. Localized delivery services provide buyers and sellers with a good customer experience through its own channels. However, the prices of international express are higher, especially in remote areas.

跨境电商卖家常用的另一种物流模式为国际快递。曾经的四大国际快递巨头为中外运敦豪、联合包裹、联邦快递和TNT。2017年,联邦快递完成了对老牌荷兰公司TNT的收购,继后,四大国际快递巨头正式变为三大,集中度进一步加强。国际快递具有时效性高、丢包率低等优点,通过自有的渠道进行本地化派送服务,为买家和卖家提供了良好的客户体验。然而,国际快递价格较高,尤其在偏远地区的附加费更高。

DHL is headquartered in Germany and is a subsidiary of the world-renowned postal and logistics group Deutsche Post DHL. In 1969, DHL opened their first express delivery route from San Francisco to Honolulu, and they expanded their routes to Japan, the Philippines, Australia and Singapore, etc. In the mid to late 1970s, DHL Airways expanded its routes to South America, the Middle East and Africa. At present, DHL's business has covered more than 220 countries and regions. In addition to basic logistics services, it provides customers with a full range of logistics solutions from document to supply chain management. In December 2018, DHL was nominated for the World's 500 Most Influential Brands. As shown in Figure 4-2, DHL has a price advantage in transporting goods under 5.5kg to the Americas and Britain. There is a separate price list for goods over 21kg.

中外运敦豪总部位于德国,是全球著名的邮递和物流集团 Deutsche Post DHL 旗下公司。1969年,它们开设了自己的第一条从旧金山到檀香山的速递运输航线,然后,它们把航线扩张到了日本、菲律宾、澳大利亚和新加坡等地。20世纪70年代中后期,敦豪航空货运公司把航线扩展到南美洲、中东地区和非洲。目前,中外运敦豪的业务已经覆盖了220多个国家和地区,除基本的物流服务外,还会为客户提供从文件到供应链管理的全系列的物流解决方案。2018年12月,中外运敦豪入围2018世界品牌500强。中外运敦豪的官网如图4-2所示。用它们运送5.5千克以下的货物到美洲、英国有价格优势,运送21千克以上的货物有单独的大货价格。

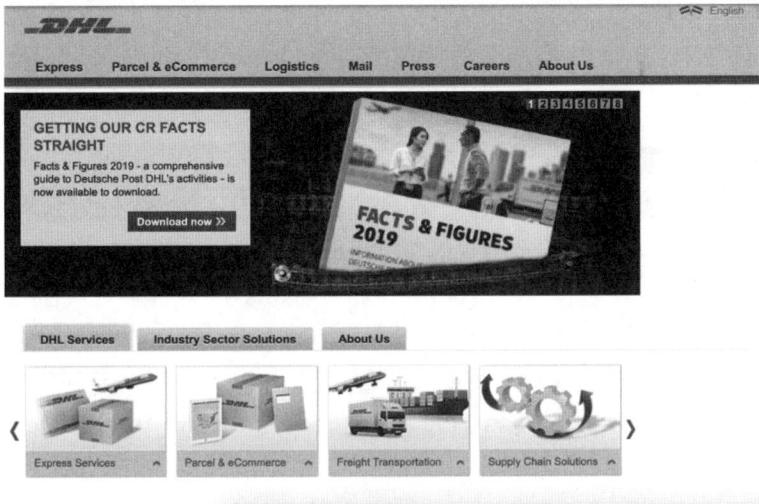

Figure 4-2（图4-2）

Founded in Washington, USA, United Parcel Service (UPS) is the world's largest express carrier and package delivery company, and a leading provider of transportation, logistics, capital and e-commerce services. UPS manages logistics, capital flow and information flow in more than 200 countries and regions around the world every day. UPS's business services have now expanded to other transportation-related areas, including integrated supply chain management, such as Nike's warehousing services and Toshiba's maintenance support services. UPS ranked the 132nd in the Fortune Global 500 released in 2019. The official website of UPS is shown in Figure 4-3. UPS is very fast for products shipped to the United States, and it is suitable for transporting 6–21 kg items to Americas and Britain.

美国联合包裹成立于美国华盛顿州,是世界上最大的快递承运商与包裹递送公司,同时也是运输、物流、资本与电子商务服务的领导性的提供者。它每天都在世界200多个国家和地区管理着物流、资金流与信息流。其业务服务已扩展到了其他与运输相关的范围,其中包括一体化的供应链管理,比如为耐克提供仓储服务和对东芝提供维修支持的服务。

美国联合包裹在2019年发布的《财富》世界500强中位列第132位。美国联合包裹的官网如图4-3所示。使用美国联合包裹发往美国速度极快，而且适合运送6—21千克的物品到美洲和英国。

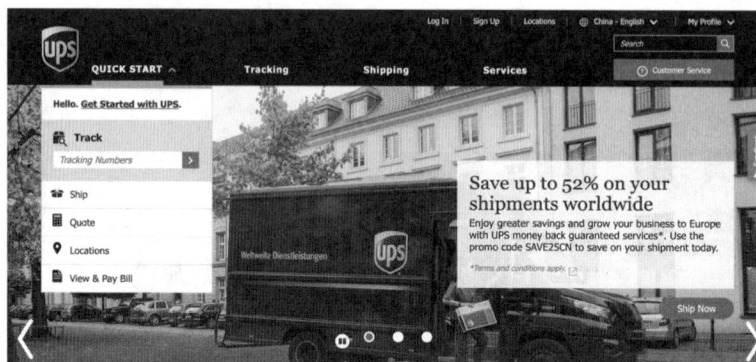

Figure 4-3（图4-3）

The full name of FedEx is Federal Express. It is headquartered in the United States with 425,000 employees and more than 220 countries and regions in the network. It is the world's largest logistics company and is affiliated with FedEx Corp. The FedEx business is divided into FedEx International Priority and FedEx International Economy. FedEx International Priority Service provides 2-5 business days services for more than 200 countries and regions around the world. FedEx International Economy service provides 4-6 business days services to more than 90 countries and regions around the world, and the price is relatively favorable. In December 2014, FedEx agreed to acquire reverse logistics company Genco, saying that FedEx will enter the e-commerce field. In May 2017, FedEx completed the acquisition of TNT, an express company with 70 years' history, for $4.8 billion, which had a huge impact on the global express delivery structure. In July 2019, FedEx ranked the 152nd in the Fortune Global 500 released in 2019. FedEx's official website is shown in Figure 4-4. Using FedEx to send more than 21kg items to Asian countries is relatively faster, but the cost is also higher.

联邦快递全称为 Federal Express，总部位于美国，拥有42.5万名员工，网络覆盖220多个国家和地区，是全球最具规模的物流公司，隶属于美国联邦快递集团。联邦快递业务分为联邦快递优先型服务和联邦快递经济型服务。联邦快递优先型服务物流时效为2—5个工作日，可为全球200多个国家和地区提供服务。联邦快递经济型服务物流时效为4—6个工作日，价格相对优惠，可为全球90多个国家和地区提供服务。2014年12月，美国联邦快递公司同意收购逆向物流公司Genco，并表示联邦快递将涉足电子商务领域。2017年5月，联邦快递以48亿美元完成对有着70年历史的老牌快递公司TNT的收购，对全球快递格局产生了巨大影响。2019年7月，联邦快递在2019年发布的《财富》世界500强中位列第152位。联邦快递的官网如图4-4所示。使用联邦快递运送21千克以上的物件到亚洲国家速度较快，但成本也比较高。

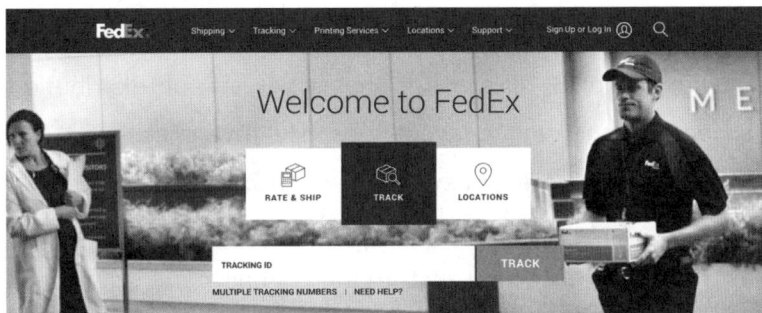

Figure 4-4（图4-4）

The full name of TNT is Thomas National Transport. It is headquartered in the Netherlands, with 150,000 employees in more than 200 countries and regions. The official website is shown in Figure 4-5. TNT's customs clearance speed is extremely fast. It only takes three days for goods to be sent to Western European countries, which ranks top among the four international express companies. It is also convenient for electronic inquiry and quick in solving problems.

TNT 的全称是 Thomas National Transport，总部位于荷兰，拥有15万名员工，分布在200多个国家和地区。其官网如图4-5所示。TNT的通关速度特别快，发往西欧国家的货物仅需要三天，时效性是四大国际快递之最，并且电子查询方便，处理问题及时。

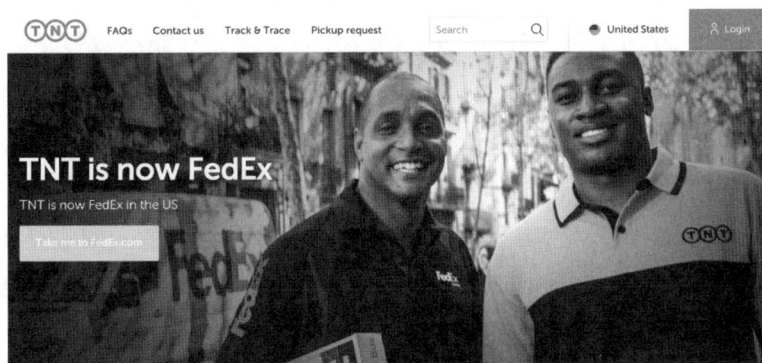

Figure 4-5（图4-5）

## 3. International Logistic Service of Domestic Express Companies （国内快递的跨境物流业务）

With the development of cross-border e-commerce, the domestic express delivery company SF and five major express companies (YTO Express, STO Express, ZTO Express, Best Express and Yunda) also joined the tide of cross-border logistics.

随着跨境电商的发展,国内的快递公司顺丰和"四通一达"也加入了跨境物流的大潮。

The main advantage of SF Express is that it has a wide distribution of domestic branches, advanced management concepts, service awareness and relatively mature business. SF Express opened economy parcel services for European countries, the United States, Russia, and Australia, and the price is also competitive. SF Express also cooperates with the local post in terms of small parcel services to enjoy the advantages of local postal clearance and distribution. It can be sent to Europe for 5–10 working days. The delivery time for order from the United States and Canada is 7–12 working days, and the timeliness is better than ordinary post parcels. The charge is close to the postal parcel, which provides an ideal selection for cross-border e-commerce sellers. Among the five major express companies, STO Express was relatively early, and US STO Express was launched in March 2014. YTO Express started cooperation with CJ Korea Express in April 2014, while ZTO Express, Best Express and Yunda are just beginning in cross-border logistics business. Domestic express delivery is faster, and the price is lower than the four international express giants. However, due to the late start and lack of relevant market experience, the overseas markets covered are currently limited.

顺丰国际快递的主要优势在于国内网点分布广、管理理念先进、服务意识强、业务相对成熟。顺丰开通了欧洲小包、美国小包、俄罗斯小包、澳大利亚小包等经济小包,价格也具有一定竞争力。顺丰和本土邮政也有合作的小包,能享受本土邮政的优先清关、配送等优势。发往欧洲5—10个工作日即可投妥,发往美国、加拿大7—12个工作日投妥,时效优于普通小包,收费接近邮政小包,为广大跨境电商卖家提供了一项理想的选择。在"四通一达"中,申通的布局相对较早,美国申通是在2014年3月上线的。圆通是2014年4月与CJ大韩通运展开合作的,而中通、汇通、韵达则是刚刚开始启动跨境物流业务。国内快递的运送速度较快,价格低于四大国际快递巨头,但是由于起步晚、缺乏相关的市场经验,覆盖的海外市场目前比较有限。

## 4. Special Line Mode (专线物流模式)

Cross-border special line logistics is a new type of cross-border logistics mode generated under the background of cross-border e-commerce development, and its scale has also expanded with the development of cross-border e-commerce. Special line logistics generally refers to the centralized transportation of goods through air cabin to other countries, and then ask local cooperative companies to distribute the products. In the case of sufficient cargo, special line logistics can reduce logistics costs through economies of scale. The timeliness and cost of special line logistics are between postal parcel and international express, with low packet loss rate and guaranteed customs clearance. Special line logistics can only meet the needs of certain market and thus has obvious regional limitations. The international special lines mainly include aviation special lines, port special lines, railway special lines, continental bridge special lines and fixed multimodal transport lines. At this stage, the most widely used cross-border logistics services in the industry include European special lines, US special lines, Australian special lines and Russian special lines, and some companies have launched special line logistics in the Middle East, South America and South Africa.

跨境专线物流是跨境电商发展背景下产生的一种新型的跨境物流模式,规模也随着跨境电商的发展不断扩大。专线物流的运送方式一般是通过航空包舱方式把货物大批量集中运送到海外,再通过合作公司进行当地的派送。在货量充足的情况下,专线物流可以通过规模效应降低物流成本。专线物流的时效性和成本都介于邮政小包和国际快递之间,丢包率低且保证清关。专线物流只能满足跨境电商比较集中的固定市场,具有明显的区域局限性。国际物流专线主要包括航空专线、港口专线、铁路专线、大陆桥专线以及固定多式联运专线。现阶段,业内使用最多的跨境专线物流产品包括欧洲专线、美国专线、澳洲专线和俄罗斯专线等,也有公司推出了中东、南美和南非等专线物流。

AliExpress first opened the Special Line-YW in cooperation with Yanwen Logistics, mainly targeting the online aviation special lines in the markets of Brazil and Russia. The South American Special Line-YW directly fly to Europe by adjusting flight resources, and then use the characteristic that the flight from Europe to South America usually carry less cargo. Then it quickly transits and shortens logistics time. The internal systems of Russian Special Line-YW parcel and Russian cooperation company are interconnected. The entire process can be visually tracked and the delivery time in Russia is within 15-25 days.

速卖通先与燕文物流合作开通了燕文专线，主要针对巴西与俄罗斯市场的线上发货航空专线。燕文南美专线小包通过调整航班资源先直飞欧洲，再发挥欧洲到南美航班货量少的特点，能实现快速中转，缩短物流时间。燕文俄罗斯专线小包与俄罗斯合作公司实现系统内部互联，全程可视化跟踪，在俄罗斯境内派送时间在15—25天。

In December 2014, AliExpress added a new Speedup-Finland postal line, which is available within the reach of post offices throughout Russia and Belarus. In July and November 2015, AliExpress added a new Spanish special line and a British special line. Only for a few cities, the goods are collected free of charge. The sellers in other areas need to ship the products to the warehouse.

2014年12月，速卖通又新增了速优宝—芬兰邮政专线，运送范围为俄罗斯及白俄罗斯全境邮局可到达的范围。2015年7月与11月，速卖通又新增了西班牙物流专线和英国专线，仅针对少数城市免费收货，其余地区的卖家需要自行发货到集货仓。

At present, Cainiao Expedited Economy is a combination of the Cainiao network and the destination country postal. It is an economical special-line service for small items up to 2kg, less than 5 dollars. It currently supports more than ten European countries including Bulgaria, Croatia, Czech Republic, Estonia, France, Germany, Britain, as well as South Korea. The Cainiao Super Economy for Special Goods service is an economical postal service for small special items (liquid, powder, paste, etc.) under 2kg. It is currently only shipped to Russia, Czech Republic, France, Germany, Britain, Italy, Netherlands, Poland, Spain and Belgium. It is only available for orders within $2 to Russia and within $5 to Europe.

目前，菜鸟专线经济是菜鸟网络与目的国邮政联合，针对2千克以下、5美元以内（含）的小件物品推出的经济类专线平邮产品，目前支持保加利亚、克罗地亚、捷克、爱沙尼亚、法国、德国、英国、韩国等10余个国家。菜鸟特货经济专线则是针对2千克以下小件特殊货品（液体、粉末、膏状等）推出的经济类邮政产品，目前只运送到俄罗斯、捷克、法国、德国、英国、意大利、荷兰、波兰、西班牙和比利时，仅限俄罗斯方向2美元以内及欧洲方向5美元以内的订单使用。

As AliExpress has developed rapidly in Africa during the recent years, especially in the wig retail market, AliExpress has also indicated that it will establish a cross-border line between China and Africa in conjunction with Cainiao, which will reduce the delivery time of wigs from an average of 30-40 days to an average of 5-7 days.

由于速卖通近几年在非洲发展迅速，尤其是假发零售市场，速卖通还表示将联合菜鸟建立中非之间的跨境专线,使假发物流时效从平均30—40天缩短到平均5—7天。

## 5. Overseas Warehouse Service Mode (国际海外仓模式)

International overseas warehouse refers to the establishment of overseas warehouses in the destination countries. The goods are first stored in the warehouse of the destination country by sea, land, air or intermodal transport, then sold through the Internet, sort and packag from overseas warehouses after receiving orders and finally deliver the products. Overseas warehouses mainly include three parts: transportation from home country to warehouse, warehouse management and local distribution. With the overseas warehouse mode, cross-border e-commerce export enterprises can save time to ship products from their home countries, reduce logistics costs, better provide localized value-added services to overseas customers, improve customer consumption stickiness, and benefit overseas markets' expansion.

国际海外仓指在销售目的国建立海外仓库,通过海运、陆运、空运或者联运的形式先把商品储存到目的国的仓库,然后通过互联网进行销售,接到订单后从海外仓库进行分拣、包装、发货与配送。海外仓主要包括头程运输、仓储管理和本地配送三个部分。利用海外仓模式,跨境电商出口企业可以节省从本国发货物流所需要的时间,降低物流成本,更好地为海外客户提供本土化增值服务,提高客户消费黏性,有利于海外市场的拓展。

In recent years, many logistics service providers and cross-border e-commerce platforms have leased or built their own overseas warehouses. As of 2018, 158 overseas companies in 33 countries and regions owned 353 warehouses, including overseas warehouses in the United States, Britain and Germany. Amazon has built 90 warehousing centers around the world to provide FBA services; eBay and Winit launched Winit overseas warehouses; Wish and CK1 jointly established US overseas warehouses; AliExpress established 9 warehouses overseas in the United States, Britain, Spain and other countries. Dalong Website has deployed overseas warehouses in Russia, Ukraine, India and other countries to serve cross-border e-commerce SMEs. FocalPrice is mainly engaged in two major categories of mobile phones and tablets. It also builds overseas warehouses in the United States. It cooperates with local logistics companies to achieve local distribution. The delivery process only takes 1-3 days.

近几年,不少物流服务商和跨境电商平台纷纷租赁或自建海外仓。截至2018年,33个国家和地区的158家海外企业拥有353个仓库,其中以位于美国、英国和德国的海外仓居多。亚马逊在全球自建90个仓储中心,提供代发货服务;易贝联合万邑通推出Winit海外仓;Wish携手出口易建立美国的海外仓;速卖通在美国、英国、西班牙等国设立了9个海外仓。大龙网在俄罗斯、乌克兰、印度等国布局海外仓,旨在服务跨境电商中小企业。FocalPrice主营手机和平板电脑两大品类,也在美国自建海外仓,通过跟美国本土物流企业合作,实现本地配送,从发货到消费者收货只需要1—3天时间。

Overseas warehouses are more suitable for goods that are expensive, bulky, and difficult to transport by traditional logistics. The rental, construction and operation of overseas warehouses require professional personnel and funds, and also have high requirements for the seller's supply chain management and inventory control. Moreover, the seller must have accurate sales expectations for the goods, otherwise there will be overstocked inventory caused by slow sales after the goods are shipped.

海外仓比较适合价格高、体积大、传统物流途径不易运输的商品。海外仓的租赁、建设与运营需要专业的人员与资金,对卖家的供应链管理、库存管控等都有较高的要求。此外,卖家对商品要有准确的销售预期,否则会在商品运送后因滞销而造成库存积压。

## 6. Fourth Party Logistics Mode (第四方物流模式)

Fourth Party Logistics refers to logistics planning, consulting, logistics information systems, supply chain management and other services for trading parties and third-party logistics. It provides comprehensive supply chain solutions by deploying its own resources and externally harmonized resources, capabilities and technologies. The Fourth Party Logistics was first proposed by Accenture Consulting in the United States in 1998 and was called the "super manager" among logistics providers. It differs from third-party logistics in that it provides a complete supply chain for marketing, transportation and distribution through its own information technology, integration capabilities and other resources to meet the needs of value-added services for cross-border e-commerce enterprises, in order to get a certain profit. In January 2015, LightInTheBox announced that it has officially launched the "Lanting Intelligence" global cross-border logistics open platform. By integrating logistics service providers around the world, it provides sellers with a series of comprehensive services including open price bidding, global intelligent path optimization, multi-logistics collaborative distribution, automatic order printing and documentary, as well as big data intelligent analysis.

第四方物流指专门为交易双方和第三方物流提供物流规划、咨询、物流信息系统、供应链管理等服务,通过调配其自身资源及外部可协调的资源、能力和技术,提供综合、全面的供应链解决方案。第四方物流是1998年由美国埃森哲咨询公司率先提出的,被其称为物流供应商中的"超级经理人"。它区别于第三方物流之处在于它通过拥有的信息技术、整合能力以及其他资源提供一套搭建营销、运输及配送等内容的完整供应链,满足广大跨境电商企业对增值服务的需求,以此获取一定的利润。2015年1月,兰亭集势宣布正式启动"兰亭智通"全球跨境物流开放平台,通过整合全球各地物流配送服务商,为卖家提供开放的比价竞价、全球智能路径优化、多物流商协同配送、自动打单跟单、大数据智能分析等一系列综合服务。

## Section Three / Selection of Cross-Border Logistics
### 跨境物流选择

Among the cross-border logistics modes in the above section, the earlier and more commonly used modes are postal parcels and international express, and they are the mainstream cross-border logistics modes. Overseas warehouses benefit from their logistics speed and the convenience of returning goods and develop quickly. It is divided into online delivery and offline delivery according to whether the product is directly delivered by cross-border e-commerce platform. Compared with offline delivery, sellers can enjoy more protection policies, avoid low logistics scores and improve account performance if they choose online delivery. However, sellers who choose offline delivery with cooperation may get relatively favorable price. For a novice seller, after understanding the characteristics of major cross-border logistics modes and major logistics service providers, how should he choose a suitable cross-border logistics mode based on the characteristics of the goods, the destination country or region, and his own capabilities?

在上述跨境物流模式中,使用较早且范围较广的是邮政小包和国际快递,两者是目前主流的跨境物流模式。海外仓得益于其物流速度及退换货的便利性,使用率正在快速上升。根据选择的物流渠道是否是跨境电商平台后台直接发货,跨境物流发货方式又分为线上发货和线下发货。线上发货相比线下发货,卖家可享受更多保护政策,规避物流低分,提高账户表现;而卖家如果选择有合作关系的渠道进行线下发货,也许可以拿到相对优惠的价格。对于一名新手卖家,在了解了各大跨境物流模式的特点及主要物流服务商之后,应该如何根据商品特点、目的国或地区以及自身能力选择适合的跨境物流模式呢?

## 1. Select Packaging and Logistics Mode According to Product Characteristics (根据商品特性进行包装及物流模式的选择)

First of all, the seller should choose different packaging materials and packaging methods according to the type, material, shape and specification of the product, considering both the safety of shipping and the cost of packaging. Common packaging materials are bubble envelopes, bubble film, corrugated boxes, packaging bags, pearl cotton, air bags and so on. For fragile goods, sellers can choose a lightweight filling material such as air cushion or foam to increase the buffer during transportation. It is better to write the words "Fragile. Handle with care." in the eye-catching position of the package to remind the delivery staff to handle it with care during transportation.

首先,卖家要根据商品的类型、材质、形状和规格选用不同的包装材料与包装方式。既考虑运送的安全性,又兼顾包装成本。常见的包装材料有气泡信封、气泡膜、瓦楞纸箱、包装袋、珍珠棉、气柱袋等。针对易碎商品,卖家可以选择气垫或者泡沫等轻便的填充材料以增加运输途中的缓冲,并在包装醒目位置写上"易损物品,轻拿轻放"等字样来提醒配送员在运输途中加以注意。

Secondly, all major cross-border logistics modes have restrictions for weight, size and value of goods. Cross-border e-commerce sellers need to choose a safe and feasible logistics mode based on the characteristics of the goods. For example, if the postal parcel has a weight limit of 4 kg, merchandise with more than 4 kg must be split into multiple pieces. EMS requires that the merchandise sent to any country could not exceed 110 cm. Economic parcels can only deliver goods within 5 dollars. Some logistics companies will regard goods with batteries as embargoed items. Relatively large pieces of furniture or large household appliances are difficult to distribute by air, and the traditional shipping method takes too long, so they are suitable for overseas warehouses.

其次,各大跨境物流模式对商品的重量、尺寸、订单金额均有适用范围,跨境电商卖家需要从商品本身的特性出发,选择安全、可行的物流模式。如邮政小包限重4千克,超过4千克的商品必须被拆分成多件;中国邮政速递物流限制寄往任何国家的商品单边不能超过110厘米;经济小包一般只能运送5美元以内的商品;部分物流公司会把带有电池的商品列为禁运物品;比较大件的家具或大型家电难以通过空运的方式配送且传统海运方式配送的时间较长,适合选择海外仓。

## 2. Select Logistics Mode According to Country or Region (根据国家或地区选择物流模式)

Some large-scale cross-border e-commerce platforms such as AliExpress, have opened special logistics lines for popular countries or regions. The special logistics line has certain advantages in terms of timeliness and cost, and the cost performance is the highest compared to international parcels and commercial express. The size and quality requirements are the same as for international parcels. SMEs can make full use of these special logistics lines and choose a cost-effective line for the distribution of goods. The special logistics line provides door-to-door collection services for some cities in China. The sellers from other cities need to send the goods to the warehouse first, and finally send the goods to the consumers according to the order information.

一些大型跨境电商平台如速卖通等针对跨境电商热门国家或地区开设了物流专线，物流专线在时效性和成本方面具有一定的优势，性价比相对于国际小包与商业快递是最高的，在尺寸和质量方面的要求与国际小包相同。中小企业可以充分利用这些物流专线，选择高性价比的专线进行商品配送。物流专线针对国内部分城市提供上门揽收服务，其余城市的卖家需要先把商品寄送至揽收仓库，最后根据订单将货物寄至消费者手中。

## 3. Select Logistics Mode According to Consumer Demand (根据消费者需求选择物流模式)

Cross-border e-commerce sellers must clearly identify the characteristics of different logistics modes to buyers before the transaction, and provide diversified logistics modes for consumers to choose under the conditions of safety, timeliness and customs clearance capacity. Consumers have different preference of logistics timeliness and cost. Sellers can set custom logistics templates based on the cost and convenience of each logistics. For example, if the cost of economic parcel is $3, while the cost is $11 with international express, the seller can set free shipping if the buyer chooses economic parcel, while the buyer who chooses international express can enjoy 10% discount of the standard shipping fee. In this way, consumers who have high time requirements can choose commercial express, while consumers who are more price sensitive can choose economic parcels. AliExpress's logistics network rules also stipulate that the logistics method selected by the seller for shipment must be the logistics mode selected by the buyer. The logistics method can never be changed without buyer's consent.

跨境电商卖家在售前要向买家明确不同物流模式的特点,在满足安全性、时效性和清关能力等条件的情况下,以尽可能地提供多样化的物流模式供消费者选择。消费者对物流时效性、费用的敏感性千差万别,卖家可以根据各项物流所需的成本与寄送便利程度设置自定义的物流模板。比如,如果卖家寄送经济小包的成本为3美元,而寄送国际快递需支付11美元,卖家可以设置减免运费配送的条件:如果买家选择经济小包可以享受包邮服务,而选择国际快递的买家则可以享受标准运费减免10%。这样,对时间要求高的消费者可以选择商业快递,而对价格更为敏感的消费者则可以选择经济小包。速卖通的物流网规也规定卖家发货所选用的物流方式必须是买家所选择的物流模式,未经买家同意,不得无故更改物流方式。

## 4. Select the Optimal Logistics Mode Based on Risk with Flexibility (根据风险灵活选择最优物流方案)

In order to meet the needs of consumers, in addition to choosing logistics models with low logistics costs, sellers should also consider other risk factors, such as risk of damage and loss. Cross-border e-commerce logistics often requires multiple transshipments, which are prone to damage, loss, etc. No matter which logistics mode is chosen, there is a certain loss rate, and the postal packet has the highest loss rate. The seller needs to measure the loss rate of each logistics mode, the upper limit of the payment and the value of the goods to select the optimal logistics mode. In general, when the value of the products are higher, sellers have to choose a logistics mode with low loss rate and high payout limit to reduce the economic losses caused by lost items. For best-selling products with high turnover and high value, sellers can also choose overseas warehouses, because high-quality overseas warehouse services can reduce the loss rate to a very low level, and will not generate excessive storage costs.

在满足消费者需求的情况下,卖家除了尽量选择物流成本低的物流模式以外,也应该综合考虑其他风险因素,比如破损丢件风险。跨境电商物流经常需要多次转运,很容易出现破损、丢失等问题,无论选择哪种物流模式,都存在一定的丢件率,其中以邮政小包的丢件率最高。卖家需要衡量各物流模式的丢件率、赔付上限和寄送商品的价值来选择最优的物流模式。一般来说,商品价值越高,卖家越要选择丢件率低、赔付上限高的物流模式,以降低丢件带来的经济损失。针对周转率高、价值高的畅销品,卖家也可以选择海外仓进行发货,因为优质的海外仓服务可以把丢件率降到很低,而且也不会产生过高的仓储成本。

At the same time, sellers should also consider the risk of full warehouses during the peak season of cross-border e-commerce, especially in the fourth quarter of each year. Thus, sellers should use different logistics methods with flexibility according to season. For example, during off-season, sellers can use the China Post package to reduce logistics costs. During peak seasons or promotional periods, sellers can use China Hongkong Post or Singapore Post to guarantee timeliness and avoid complaints caused by package accumulation and delayed delivery.

同时,卖家也要考虑跨境电商旺季的爆仓风险,尤其是每年的第四个季度。卖家需根据淡旺季灵活使用不同物流方式。例如,在淡季时卖家可以使用中国邮政小包降低物流成本,而旺季或者大型促销活动期间,卖家可以采用中国香港邮政或者新加坡邮政来保证时效,以避免因快递堆积、延迟送达而导致的投诉。

## Section Four / Extensive Reading: China Railway Express
拓展阅读:中欧班列

With economic globalization, the dependency of Central European economy on other countries is increasing due to its huge complementarity. Currently, China is the EU's second largest export market and the largest import market. In 2014, China-EU trade volume reached 615.1 billion dollars, accounting for 14.3% of China's total import and export volume. Under the condition of global economic downturn in 2015, China-EU trade relations developed steadily, and the trade volume between China and EU reached 574.7 billion dollars. With the continuous development of China-EU trade, a number of direct container railway trains have been started to operate in many parts of China since 2011.

随着经济全球化,中欧经济由于其巨大的互补性,对其他国家的依存度越来越高。目前,中国是欧盟第二大出口市场和第一大进口市场。2014年,中欧贸易额达6151亿美元,占中国进出口总额的14.3%。2015年在全球经济低迷的大环境下,中欧贸易关系稳定发展,中国与欧盟的货物贸易额达5747亿美元。随着中欧贸易的不断发展,自2011年,我国多个地区开通了多条直达欧洲的集装箱货运班列。

China Railway Express refers to the international container railway transit express between China, Europe and the countries along "the Belt and Road", which is opened under the conditions of fixed trains and routes. By taking advantage of the short distance of international railway, CRexpress can transport higher value-added products to Europe by railway. Due to its high speed, high security, short time, environmentally protection, and limited impact from the natural environment, China Railway Express has provided new option for Eurasia's cargo transportation, which is of great significance for strengthening China-European trade relations.

中欧班列是指按照固定车次、线路等条件开行,往来于中国与欧洲及"一带一路"沿线各国的集装箱国际铁路联运班列。中欧班列通过发挥国际铁路运输的距离较短的优势,将附加值较高的产品以班列的形式运往欧洲等地。由于具有速度快、安全性高、运行时间短、绿色环保以及受自然环境影响小等优势,中欧班列为欧亚大陆的货物运输提供了新的运输选择,对加强中欧贸易关系意义重大。

China Railway Express has 3 lines in the west, the middle and the east: the west line exits from the Midwest of China via Alataw pass (Khorgos); the middle line exits from North China via Erlianhot; and the east line exits from southeastern coastal area via Manchuria (Suifen River). By the end of June 2018, the cumulative number of China Railway Express had exceeded 9,000 with nearly 800,000 TEUs of goods, with 48 domestic cities and 42 international cities in 14 countries in Europe. The transportation network covers the major areas of Asia and Europe. Among them, YIXINOU China-Europe Railway has already opened 10 lines in 35 countries, becoming the highest-ranking China Railway Express in the country.

中欧班列铺划了西中东3条运行线:西部通道由我国中西部经阿拉山口(霍尔果斯)出境,中部通道由我国华北地区经二连浩特出境,东部通道由我国东南部沿海地区经满洲里(绥芬河)出境。截至2018年6月底,中欧班列累计开行量已突破9000列,运送货物近80万标箱,国内开行城市48个,到达欧洲14个国家42个城市,运输网络覆盖亚欧大陆的主要区域。其中,"义新欧"班列已经开通了10条线路,辐射面达到35个国家,成为全国市场化贸易程度最高的中欧班列。

The logistics organization of China Railway Express has become increasingly mature. The economic and trade between the countries along the route have become increasingly active. The cooperation on railway, ports and customs among countries has become increasingly close. The well-planned China Railway Express will not only bring benefits to countries and railway transportation groups, but more importantly, it can be used as a new transportation and logistics option to allocate local resources, and to improve the logistics capacity of inland cities. It will add new possibilities to economic globalization to the world due to its mutual integration and interoperability.

中欧班列物流组织日趋成熟,班列沿途国家经贸交往日趋活跃,国家间铁路、口岸、海关等部门的合作日趋紧密。规划合理的中欧班列不仅能为各国、铁路运输集团带来一定收益,更重要的是中欧班列作为新的运输和物流配置方式可以调配各地资源,提升内陆城市的物流运输能力,兼容并包、互融互通,为世界经济全球化增添新的可能性。

# Chapter Five

## Customer Service of Cross-Border E-Commerce

跨境电商客服

/ **Lead-in**

导入

Being close to consumers, cross-border e-commerce customer service can help consumers understand product features, functions, as well as getting after-sales feedback and support. It plays an important role in improving store evaluation, increasing consumer stickiness and core competitiveness of enterprises. The American Express survey shows that 90% of Americans use customer service as a factor in deciding whether to do business with a company. And consumers are willing to spend 17% more on a company with excellent customer service. Therefore, it's necessary for cross-border sellers who need to expand overseas markets to strive to provide localized and personalized customer service to customers in the target market to increase product added value and achieve sustainable management. This chapter will introduce the position features, required skills, after-sales service and customer relationship management of cross-border customer service.

跨境电商客服作为跨境电商的窗口工作,能够帮助消费者了解产品特性、功能,获得售后反馈以及支持,对提升店铺的评价、增加消费者黏性以及企业核心竞争力起着重要的作用。美国运通公司调查显示90%的美国人把客户服务作为决定是否与一家公司做生意的一个因素,而且消费者愿意为一家拥有卓越的客户服务的公司多花17%的钱。因此,对于需要拓展海外市场的跨境卖家,必须努力为目标市场的客户提供本土化和个性化的客户服务,以增加产品附加值,实现可持续经营。本章会依次介绍跨境客服的岗位特点、所需技能、售后服务和客户关系管理等内容。

## Section One / **Overview of Cross-Border Customer Service**

跨境客服概述

### 1. Responsibilities of Cross-Border Customer Service（跨境客服的工作内容）

The main tasks of cross-border customer service include pre-sales consultation, sales follow-up, after-sales services, in order to prevent possible disputes, properly resolving various disputes that have arisen, and maximally protect the company's interests. In addition, cross-border customer service personnel also need to assist in collating product data based on communication with consumers, summarizing product issues and proposing product optimization recommendations. In addition, cross-border customer service personnel need to process orders in time, upload and remove products at regular intervals, edit products and optimize product information, pay attention to unpaid orders and communicate with customers, deal with account-related issues in time and keep accounts running smoothly.

跨境客服的主要工作内容包括售前咨询、售中跟进、售后处理等,预防可能出现的争议,妥善解决各种已出现的争议,最大限度地维护公司利益。另外,跨境客服也需要根据与消费者的沟通内容协助整理产品数据,汇总产品问题,提出产品优化建议。除此之外,跨境客服还需要及时处理订单,定时上传及下架产品,编辑产品并优化商品信息,关注未付款的订单并与客户进行沟通,及时处理账号相关的问题,保持账号平稳运营等。

In the process of pre-sales consultation, cross-border e-commerce customer service personnel should receive customers politely and professionally. And they should enthusiastically answer customer-related consultations on products, payment methods, logistics and after-sales service, so that customers can fully understand the products and dispel all concerns, as well as guide customers to successfully complete payments. When the service attitude and quality can touch overseas customers and win their praise, the mutual trust relationship will prompt customers to continuously repurchase orders in the future. Customers will even recommend their stores to their friends and family through social media, which can greatly enhance the store's page views and brand awareness.

在售前咨询的过程中,跨境电商客服要礼貌、专业地接待客户,热情地解答客户对产品、支付方式、物流、售后服务相关的咨询,让客户充分地了解产品,打消客户的所有顾虑,引导客户成功下单。当店铺提供的服务态度与质量能够感动海外客户,赢得海外客户的称赞时,这种人与人之间的相互信任关系会促使客户在未来持续地回购下单。客户甚至会通过社交媒体把店铺推荐给自己的亲友,这样可以大大提升店铺的浏览量和品牌知名度。

Since the products online cannot be seen before they arrive, they can only be judged by image, description and other users' evaluations. Before ordering, customers are more concerned about whether the product is consistent with the seller's advertising. In this case, the customer will ask the customer service personnel about the product quality, material, color, specifications, size, ways of sales, etc., via email or in-station communication tools. Customer service personnel should be proficient in the company's product-related expertise and have good promotional skills, patiently respond to them and recommend products in a targeted manner to prompt customers to order and increase conversion rates.

由于线上购物时无法看到真实商品,仅能通过图片信息、文字信息及其他用户的评价进行判断,所以在下单前客户比较关心商品是否和卖家的广告宣传一致。在这种情况下,客户会通过电子邮件或站内沟通工具询问客服人员有关产品质量、材质、颜色、规格、尺寸、产品销售方式等方面的信息。客服人员应该熟练掌握与公司产品有关的专业知识和良好的促销技能,耐心地一一回复,有针对性地推荐产品,促使客户下单并提高转化率。

For example, for common specifications and size issues, sellers generally set them to the units and forms that overseas customers are accustomed to, and specify them in the detailed product description. However, some buyers will ignore them. In case of product specifications and dimensions, the seller should repeat the specific specifications and dimensions and guide the buyer to confirm the specifications and dimensions explanation. In addition, some overseas buyers will use their usual measurement units for size consultation. Cross-border customer service personnel need to be familiar with these size conversion formulas and give appropriate recommendations. For example, a British customer will tell you that his weight is 11 stones and his height is 6 feet, and then ask you what size to choose. Cross-border customer service can convert the height and weight into 70 kg and 1.83 m, and probably make a size recommendation after understanding the customer's figure. To avoid disputes due to size, customers can also be encouraged to confirm the size through the detailed description page. These measures are of great significance to the improvement of customer experience and satisfaction.

比如,针对比较常见的产品规格和尺寸问题。卖家一般会把产品规格和尺寸设置成海外客户习惯的单位和形式,并在产品详情页描述中详细地说明产品的规格和尺寸,但也不排除部分买家会忽略产品规格和尺寸等信息。遇到产品规格和尺寸方面的询问,卖家应将产品的具体规格和尺寸进行重复,并引导买家再次确认详情页中的规格和尺寸说明。此外,一些海外买家会用他们常用的计量单位进行尺码咨询,跨境客服需要熟悉这些尺码转换公式,并给出合适的尺码推荐。比如,英国客户可能会问他的体重是11英石,身高是6英尺,他应该选哪个尺码。跨境客服需要把客户提供的体重和身高分别换算成70千克和1.83米,在大概了解了客户的身材之后再做出尺码推荐。为避免由于尺码产生的纠纷,也可以鼓励客户通过详情页的尺码设置自行确认，这些措施对客户体验和满意度的提升都有非常重大的意义。

In most cases, customers on cross-border platforms will not bargain with the seller, but some customers will negotiate the price before ordering, asking the seller for a certain discount. For these buyers, the seller should respond and deal with it according to the different situations. Sellers should pay special attention to small wholesale customers, actively follow up the inquiry and negotiate more favorable wholesale price according to the quantity in order to retain them. Periodic small wholesale orders are beneficial to the business of the store. For enquiry that involves large amount wholesale, sellers must take the opportunity and reply in detail. The content generally includes style, purchase volume and corresponding quotation. The quotation proposal includes freight. And the price should be competitive, giving the buyer the feeling of a great discount. For some retail products with considerable profit margins, sellers can also have an appropriate allowance to win the order. For example, eBay provides the seller with Best Offer, and customers can negotiate prices with sellers for products that have this feature.

在大多数情况下，跨境平台上的客户不会与卖家讨价还价，但也有部分特殊客户在下单之前会进行价格的商讨，要求卖家给予一定的折扣。关于这部分的买家，卖家应根据具体情况，有针对性地进行回复和处理。对于一些小额批发客户，卖家应给予重视，积极跟进询盘，根据批发数量商定较有优势的批发价格，争取留住这些小额批发客户，因为周期性的小额批发订单有利于店铺的良性经营。对于大量批发询盘，卖家一定要抓住机会，回复一定要详尽，内容一般包括样式、采购量和相应的报价，报价建议包括运费，而且价格要相对有优势，给买家感觉是卖家给他的一个特大优惠。而对于一些利润空间可观的零售产品，卖家也可以适当让价以赢得订单。比如，易贝平台就为卖家提供了议价功能，客户可以针对设置了这一功能的产品与卖家进行价格协商。

## 2. Skills of Cross-Border Customer Service（跨境客服的岗位技能）

Since cross-border e-commerce enterprises conduct business with overseas companies, good English listening, speaking, reading and writing skills are essential for any cross-border e-commerce customer service personnel. When recruiting employees, enterprises usually use CET-4, CET-6, IELTS, TOEFL and BEC to identify the foreign language level of candidates. In addition to good language communication skills, cross-border e-commerce customer service personnel also need to master the cultural and consumption habits of each country to cater to overseas consumers during the chat.

由于跨境电商企业是与海外企业进行业务往来的,良好的英语听、说、读、写能力是任何跨境电商客服人员必不可少的技能。企业在招聘员工时通常会用全国大学英语四级或六级证书以及雅思、托福、商务英语等证书来识别应聘者的外语水平。除了良好的语言沟通能力,跨境电商客服人员也需要掌握各国文化背景及消费习惯,以在聊天过程中迎合海外消费者。

Secondly, cross-border customer service personnel need to have a positive attitude and good communication skills. The words and deeds of cross-border customer service are closely related to the customer's feelings about the store. A customer service personnel that can understand the customer's feelings can leave customers a good impression. Any contact between the customer service personnel and consumers may bring sales growth. During the communication, customer service personnel must continue to listen to the feedback of customers, understand each other from the perspective of the other side, grasp the consumer psychology and emotions, provide humanized responses, and try to avoid automatic responses.

其次,跨境客人员服需要拥有积极的态度和良好的沟通技巧。跨境客服人员的一言一行都关系着客户对店铺的感受,一个能够将心比心理解客户感受的客服能给客户留下良好的印象,任何一次客服和消费者的接触都有可能带来销量的增长。在与客户的沟通过程中,客服人员要通过持续地倾听客户的反馈,站在对方的角度理解对方,把握客户消费心理和情绪,提供人性化的回复,尽量避免自动回复。

Finally, because cross-border customer service personnel are the closest to consumers and markets in cross-border enterprises, an excellent cross-border e-commerce customer service personnel need to have keen market insight and strong data analysis capabilities. This not only requires cross-border customer service personnel to have the ability to solve customer problems, maintain and analyze the customer's database, but also requires them to think and summarize customer feedback and problems, summarize product issues, accurately grasp users' needs and provide valuable advice for products improvement and new products development.

最后,由于跨境客服是跨境企业中离消费者、市场最近的岗位,所以一名优秀的跨境电商客服人员需要具有敏锐的市场洞察力和较强的数据分析能力。这就要求跨境客服人员不但要有解决客户问题的能力,维护及分析客户的数据库,还要善于思考和总结客户的反馈及问题,汇总产品问题,准确把握客户需求,为产品优化与新产品开发提供宝贵的建议。

# Section Two / **After-Sales Service**
## 售后服务

Cross-border e-commerce after-sales service refers to the various service activities provided by the seller after the sale of products. After-sales issues are directly related to customer experience, affecting the performance and security of the seller's account. At the same time, this is also a way of promotion. High-quality after-sales service can enhance the credibility of the enterprise and expand market share of products. The scope of after-sales service mainly includes order problems, disputes about refund and return, as well as after-sales maintenance problems.

跨境电商售后服务,指在商品出售以后卖家所提供的各种服务活动。售后问题直接关系着客户体验,影响着卖家账号的表现和安全。同时,这也是一种促销手段,优质的售后服务可以提高企业的信誉,扩大产品的市场占有率。售后服务范围主要包括订单问题、退款退货纠纷、售后维修问题等。

## 1. Problems About the Order (订单问题)

If order is not shipped, and the customer requests to modify the address due to incorrect address or other reasons, the seller can ask the customer to send the correct new address and communicate with the customer amicably to confirm again that the address is correct. Orders can also be cancelled at the customer's request.

在订单未发货的情况下,如果客户因地址填写错误或其他原因要求修改地址,卖家可以要求客户发送正确的新地址,并友好地和客户沟通进行再次确认,保证地址无误,也可以根据客户的请求取消订单。

If order has been shipped, but the customer needs to change the address and send the new address to the seller, the seller may consider resending a new product to the revised shipping address of the customer with a lower cost product. If the price of the product is high, the seller can write an e-mail to the customer, euphemistically state that the order has been shipped, it is not convenient to modify the address, and ask the customer for understanding. If the customer cancels the order after the item is issued, the seller should first contact the customer and ask why the order was cancelled. Inform the customer that the order has been shipped, the products cannot be returned. The seller should communicate with the customer amicably and ask if the customer is willing to accept the product. If the customer does not want this product, the seller can advise the customer to refuse to sign after arrival, and the seller will refund the customer.

如果订单已发货,但客户需要修改地址并把新地址发送给了卖家,针对较低成本的产品,卖家可考虑重发一个到客户的新收货地址。如果产品的价格较高,卖家可以给客户写封邮件,委婉地说明订单已发货,不便修改地址,并请求客户谅解。如果在商品发出后,客户取消订单,卖家应先联系客户,询问取消订单的原因,再告知客户订单已发货,无法追回货物,友好地和客户沟通,询问客户是否愿意接受此商品。若客户仍坚持不要此商品,到货之后建议客户拒签,卖家给客户进行退款。

In the process of cargo transportation, if the seller chooses Amazon FBA delivery, Amazon will help seller handle all customer service questions and logistics issues. The seller can advise the customer to ask Amazon customer service to provide a solution.

在货物运输过程中,如果卖家选择的是亚马逊FBA发货,亚马逊会帮卖家处理所有的客服和物流问题。卖家可以建议客户去询问亚马逊客服,让其提供解决方案。

## 2. Disputes About Refund or Return (退款退货纠纷)

A refund or return dispute is a problem that almost all companies will experience. Correctly handling these disputes can increase customer loyalty and strengthen the brand image. Conversely, it may lower the enterprise's reputation and lose valuable customers.

退款退货纠纷几乎是所有公司都会经历的问题,正确处理这些纠纷可以提高客户忠诚度,强化品牌形象。反之,可能会有损公司声誉,丢失有价值的客户。

There are three reasons for a buyer to file a refund. One is that the buyer has not received the goods; another is that the buyer receives the goods, but the goods do not conform to the agreement; and the last one is that the buyer requests a refund because of his own personal reasons.

买家提起退款申请一般有三种原因:一是买家未收到货物;二是买家收到货物,但货物与约定不符;三是由于买家自身原因申请退款。

The disputes that the buyer did not receive the goods mainly includes non-logistics information, the logistics shows the products was properly delivered but the buyer still complained that they did not receive the products, the products detained by the customs, the products were in transit, the original products were returned, and the seller changed the logistics method privately.

买家未收到货的纠纷主要涵盖查无物流信息、物流显示已妥投但买家仍投诉未收到货物、海关扣关、货物在运输途中、货物原件退回、卖家私自更改物流方式等。

No logistics information means that the waybill number filled out by the seller does not have tracking information on the logistics website. There are two cases when the logistics shows that the products have been properly delivered but the buyer still complains that the products have not been received. One case is that the logistics address matches the buyer's order address, and the logistics information shows that the products have been properly delivered, and the delivered address and person who signed match the order address and the personal information on the order. The other case is that the delivered address does not match the buyer's order address.

查无物流信息是指卖家填写的运单号在物流网站查不到跟踪信息。物流显示已妥投而买家仍投诉未收到货物,一种情况是物流妥投地址与买家下单地址匹配,即物流信息显示已妥投,且物流妥投国家与买家下单地址和签收人一致;另一种情况是物流妥投地址与买家下单地址不匹配。

Customs deduction means that logistics show that the products are in customs and the products are detained due to customs requirements of the importing country. The main reasons are: the importing country has restrictions on imported goods; the buyer is unwilling to clear the customs because of the high tariff; the products are fakes, counterfeit goods, prohibited goods; the declared value of the goods does not match the actual value; the seller cannot issue relevant documents required by the importing country; the buyer can't issue relevant documents required by the importing country and so on.

海关扣关是指物流显示货物在海关,货物由于涉及进口国海关要求而被扣留。主要原因有:进口国对进口货物有限制;买家因关税过高不愿清关;订单货物属假货、仿货、违禁品;货物申报价值与实际价值不符;卖家无法出具进口国需要的相关文件;买家无法出具进口国需要的相关文件;等等。

The goods in transit refer to the situation where the logistics tracking information on the official website of the logistics company is between "sent" and "delivered". The return of the original products means that the logistics has tracking information, and the tracking information indicates that the products have been returned. The seller has privately changed logistics method without the buyer's permission , which means that the seller uses a different logistic method from the one that is selected by the buyer when placing the order.

货物在运输途中是指包裹在物流公司官方网站的物流追踪信息介于"收寄"和货物"妥投"之间的情形。货物原件退回是指物流有跟踪信息,并且跟踪信息显示货物被退回。卖家私自更改物流方式是指未经买家允许,卖家使用与买家下单时选择的不同物流方式发货。

The products do not conform to the agreement include the products are not as same as descriptions, quality problems, sales of fakes, wrong products, short shipment, damaged products. The difference between the products and description refers to the difference of the description of the products and product detailed description page on the website and the actual products in terms of color, size, product packaging, brand, style or model. The quality problem refers to the quality and function of the products received by the buyer, such as the inability of the electronic equipment to work and the poor quality of products. The sale of counterfeit products refers to the refund of the goods after the buyer receives the goods because the goods are counterfeit products or suspected counterfeit products. Short shipment means that the quantity of products received by the buyer is less than the quantity agreed on the order. Damage to the products means that the products received by the buyer have different degrees of damage on packaging or the product itself is damaged.

货物与约定不符包括货物与描述不符、质量问题、销售假货、发错货物、货物短装、货物破损等。其中货物与描述不符是指买家收到的货物与卖家在网站相应的产品详情页面的描述存在颜色、尺寸、产品包装、品牌、款式或型号等方面的差距。质量问题是指买家所收到的货物出现品质、使用方面的问题,如电子设备无法工作、产品的质地差等。销售假货是指买家收到货物后因货物为侵权假冒产品或涉嫌侵权假冒产品而提起退款。货物短装是指买家所收到的货物数量少于订单上约定的数量。货物破损是指买家所收到的货物存在不同程度的外包装或者产品本身有损坏的情况。

There are also some disputes raised by malicious buyers or competitors, which are the most difficult customer service problems to solve. In general, if the buyer wants a partial refund, it can be done in an acceptable range. If it is a very malicious dispute, sellers can blacklist the buyer and submit the case to the platform to solve this problem.

还有一些恶意买家或者竞争对手提起的纠纷,是客服最难解决的。一般来说,如果买家想要部分退款,在可以接受的范围内,卖家可以小事化无。如果是非常过分的恶意纠纷,卖家可以将对方拉入黑名单并提交给平台处理。

Regardless of the cause of disputes, once it is submitted, there will be many effects. Not only will it affect the buyer's shopping experience, but also affect the buyer's trust in the platform. If the buyer's shopping experience is not good, the buyer will not only doubt the seller, but also indirectly doubt the credibility of the platform. Thus, they may question the platform, platform suppliers and their products, and finally creating a vicious circle. Therefore, the seller must respond to the dispute in a timely manner. If it exceeds a certain period of time, the platform will refund the buyer directly. The customer service is obliged to minimize the loss of the dispute. By measuring the dispute rate of the store and the cost of direct refund, the loss of the store refund is minimized under the premise of ensuring the safe operation of the store.

不论是什么原因引起的纠纷,一旦提起,就会有多方面的影响。这不仅会影响买家的购物体验,同时还影响着买家对平台的信任。如果购物体验不好,买家不但会对卖家的信任产生怀疑,还会间接失去对平台的信任,从而质疑平台、平台供应商和其产品,最后产生恶性循环。因此,卖家必须及时回应纠纷。如果超过一定时间,平台会直接退款给买家。客服有义务将纠纷损失降到最低,通过衡量店铺的纠纷提起率和直接退款的成本,在保证店铺安全运营的前提下把店铺退款的损失降至最低。

Wish Platform has a "100% Guaranteed Buyer Satisfaction" policy, that is, buyers can return goods unconditionally within 30 days after receiving the goods. If the seller does not want to accept this policy, they can make changes in refund policy in sellers' dashboard.

Wish平台有"100%保证买家满意"的政策,即买家可以在收货后30天无条件退换货。如果卖家不想接受此政策,可以在后台的退款政策中进行修改。

## 3. After-Sales Maintenance Problems (售后维修问题)

For digital and household appliances, if there is a problem during the warranty period, the seller also needs to deal with the after-sales maintenance problem. In general, there are several solutions: return to domestic factory for maintenance; send a new one to the customer; return to the overseas warehouse, find a professional team to repair in overseas warehouse; refund the customer and the customer does not return the product.

针对数码、家用电器类产品,如果在保修期间出现问题的话,卖家还需要处理售后维修问题。一般来说,有以下几种解决方案:退回国内维修;重新给顾客寄一个产品;退回海外仓,找专业团队到海外仓维修;退款不退货。

In the case of small items, sellers generally choose to reissue or refund. If the product is large in size, heavy in weight, and high in price, the return shipping cost or refund cost will be high, and many sellers will choose to return certain amount of money. If sellers want to repair, they must have an overseas warehouse, or they can find a local third-party professional team to solve the after-sales maintenance problem. If sellers have a certain strength and a high overseas market share, they can consider build overseas repair service stations on their own. The cost is higher, but it is conducive to building brand awareness. Sellers can also make the full control of service content, service quality, service timeliness, etc.

如果是小件商品,卖家一般会选择重发或者退款。如果产品体积、重量较大,成本较高,退货运费或者退款成本都会很高,很多卖家会选择退回一部分款项。如果要进行维修,那么卖家必须要有海外仓,或者可以找当地第三方专业团队解决售后维修的问题。如果拥有一定的实力和较高的海外市场占有率,卖家可以考虑自建海外维修服务站。虽然这样成本较高,但是有利于打造品牌的知名度,卖家也可以对服务内容、服务质量、服务时效等做到全方位的掌控。

Whether it is Amazon or other cross-border e-commerce platforms, in the final analysis, it is necessary to start with good product quality, reduce the possibility of product problems, and thus reduce subsequent after-sales costs.

无论是亚马逊还是其他跨境电商平台,归根结底还是要从产品质量入手,降低产品出现问题的可能性,减少后续的售后成本。

## Section Three / **Customer Relationship Management**
## 客户关系管理

In business models, a single transaction brings profit only once to the business. In order for the buyer and the seller to obtain sustained profits through long-term transactions, efforts must be made to create a strong bond between the buyer and the seller. This is not only a continuous value, but also an added value, because this stickiness can produce new values such as brand value and service value that are not related to the transaction itself.

在商业模式中,单次的交易给商业带来的仅仅是单次的利润,为了让买卖双方通过长期的交易获得持续的利润,就必须努力使买卖双方形成强大的黏性。这不但是价值的持续体现,更是价值的增值,因为这个黏性继而产生诸如品牌价值、服务价值等与交易本身无关的新的价值。

Customer relationship management refers to the enterprise's ability to improve its core competitiveness, and to accurately contact, segment, market, manage and maintain existing customers through big data, thereby improving its management methods and providing customers with innovative and personalized customer interactions, as well as the process of service. The ultimate goal is to attract new customers, retain regular customers, and turn existing customers into loyal customers, and increase the market share.

客户关系管理是指企业为提高核心竞争力,通过大数据对现有的客户进行精准接触、细分、营销、管理和维护,从而提升其管理方式,向客户提供创新式的、个性化的客户交互和服务的过程。其最终目标是吸引新客户、保留老客户以及将已有客户转为忠实客户,增加市场份额。

Compared with domestic customers, after having a good shopping experience, overseas customers will be more likely to be long term customers, repurchase products or share the products with their friends. Regular customers are an important asset of the enterprise. The cost of developing a new customer is 5 to 25 times to the cost of maintaining an existing customer. Moreover, compared with developing new customers, sellers do not need to spend time introducing companies and products to regular customers who have already purchased products in the store, which can save a lot of time and cost. Therefore, customer relationship maintenance is a key link that cross-border e-commerce sellers can't ignore. So, how do sellers maintain customer relationships, win customer trust, and build stickiness with their customers with the characteristics of cross-border e-commerce customers? This requires sellers to consider the basis of cross-border e-commerce platform.

相比国内客户,海外客户在店铺成交之后,一旦拥有良好的购物体验更容易产生客户黏性、回购产品或者分享给身边的朋友。老客户是企业的重要资产,投资新客户的成本是维护现有客户成本的5—25倍。并且,对于已经购买过店铺产品的老客户,卖家不需要像发展新客户那样花时间介绍公司和产品,这样可以节省不少时间成本。因此,做好客户关系维护是跨境电商卖家不可忽视的一个关键环节。那么,卖家又如何在跨境电商平台客户特点下维护客户关系、赢得客户信任、建立与客户之间的黏性呢? 这就需要卖家基于跨境电商平台的基础来考虑。

## 1. Collect Customer Data to Build Customer Database (收集客户资料建立客户数据库)

Customer service personnel should collect detailed information about the customer's basic personal information, purchase history, purchase preferences and concerns, and establish a complete customer database. These can help sellers understand all the details of customer preferences, tag them with these customer data, build users' portraits, and effectively group customers. In this way, sellers can provide personalized service to customers in the future and carry out precise marketing.

客服人员应该收集有关客户的个人基本信息、购买历史、购买偏好和顾虑等详细信息,建立起完整的客户数据库,这些"蛛丝马迹"都可以帮助卖家了解客户喜好。卖家可以通过这些客户数据为他们打上标签,构建起用户画像,有效地划分客户群体。这样,卖家后期就可以为客户提供个性化的服务,进行精准营销了。

## 2. Regularly Contact Returning Customers (定期回访老客户)

Customer service personnel can contact customers proactively. They can ask returning customers to give feedback on the quality and service of recent purchases, as well as putting forward suggestions for improvement. This practice will allow the buyer to know that the seller is truly buyer-centered, allowing the customer to understand the seller's attention to him, and to grasp the advantages and disadvantages of the product from the consumer perspective, and provide advice to product developers. In order to retain customers, many cross-border e-commerce sellers will send an e-mail or a greeting letter on holidays or customers' birthdays to maintain the contact of customers and help to follow up in the future. The following is a sample letter for returning customers to make suggestions.

客服人员可以主动联系客户,请老客户对近期产品的质量和服务进行反馈,提出改进的意见等。这样做既可以让买家知道卖家是真正以买家为中心,让客户体会到卖家对他的关注,又可以从消费者层面掌握产品的优缺点,向产品开发人员提供建议。为了留住客户,很多跨境电商卖家会在节假日或者客户生日的时候,发一封邮件或者问候的信函等等,维系与客户的情感,这将有助于后续跟进。以下是卖家希望老客户提出建议的邮件参考模板。

> Dear Mary,
>
> Thank you for your attention to our store all the time. And I am writing to ask if you have any advice or questions to our products. Please let us know and any advice will have our best and prompt attention.
>
> We look forward to your kind reply and have a nice day!
>
> Best regards,
>
> Tom Liu

## 3. Respond to Regular Customers' Emails in Time (及时回复老客户的邮件)

Regular customers' emails must be given priority, and it is best to reply on the same day. If customer service personnel encounter a problem that cannot be answered immediately and need to wait for a reply from another company or person to respond, they must also inform the customer in time. For example, they can reply like this:"The message has been received and is being processed." Even in this case, the response to regular customers must not exceed three days.

老客户的邮件一定要优先回复,最好能够在当天回复。如果客服人员碰到无法立刻解答的问题,需要等待来自其他单位或人员的答复才能准确回复的,也一定要及时告知客户。例如:"邮件已收到,正在处理中"。即便如此,对于老客户的回复也一定不要超过三天。

## 4. Set up Special Activities for Regular Customers (设置老客户活动)

Sellers can set up some special activities for returning customers, such as sending discount codes for promotional activities, lotteries, etc., so that regular customers can enjoy special VIP care and feel the preferential treatment that they cannot experience in other stores. Sellers can also invite customers with a large transaction volume to visit company, let customers feel the enthusiasm, and show the strength of the company at the same time. It will enhance customer stickiness, and then increase the opportunities for further cooperation. The following is a sample letter for sending discount codes.

卖家可以针对老客户设置一些活动,比如发放促销活动的折扣码、抽奖活动等,让老客户享受到特殊的 VIP 关怀,感受到在别的店铺体会不到的优待。卖家也可以邀请交易量比较大的客户前来参观,在让客户感受到热情的同时,也有机会向他们展示公司的实力,增强客户黏性,进而增加后期合作机会。以下是发放折扣码的邮件参考模板。

> Dear Mr. Smith,
>
> Thank you for your support of our products all the time. In order to celebrate the 5-year-anniversary of our company, we are currently offering 10% discount of all products for returning customers like you. Please use Promotion Code: VIP10 before checkout. Have a wonderful weekend.
>
> Best regards,
>
> Lily Han

## Section Four / **Extensive Reading: Intelligent Customer Service**
拓展阅读:智能客服

In general, cross-border e-commerce customer service will face problems such as time difference and language difference. The time difference problem will cause the customer service personnel to fail to respond to the buyer in time, resulting in returns of products and negative reviews. Inaccurate foreign language communication will reduce the customer's buying experience, causing buyers to question the quality of after-sales service. In addition, customer service personnel often need a certain period of training. Frequent resignation of customer service personnel will lead to the instability of after-sales service quality and waste of training costs. Therefore, many enterprises will consider using an intelligent customer service system.

一般来说,跨境电商客服会面临时差、语言等问题。时差导致客服人员无法及时回复买家,造成退货和差评。不精准的外语沟通会影响客户购买体验,导致买家质疑卖家的售后服务质量。此外,客服人员往往需要经过一段时间的培训,并且客服人员的频繁离职会导致产品售后服务不稳定,培训成本的浪费等问题,因此,不少企业会考虑使用智能客服系统。

The intelligent customer service system is an industry-oriented application developed on the basis of large-scale knowledge processing. It is applicable to technical industries like large-scale knowledge processing, natural language understanding, knowledge management, automatic question answering system, reasoning, etc. It can be online 24 hours a day, automatically reading and understanding the questions raised by buyers and providing answers. Smart Reply can solve the most common customer problems, improve the response speed of staff and help sellers solve the jet lag problem with customers. In addition, the intelligent customer service also supports one-to-many, global mainstream language dialogue services, switching multiple identities at any time. And it can transform into roles like intelligent customer service, corporate website guide, shopping assistant, discount offer extraction, questions answering, user information administrator. Therefore, the application of intelligent customer service products can save a lot of labor costs.

智能客服系统是在大规模知识处理基础上发展起来的一项面向行业的应用,适用于大规模知识处理、自然语言理解、知识管理、自动问答系统、推理等等技术行业。智能客服可以做到24小时全天候在线,自动读取和理解买家提出的问题并提供答案。智能回复可以解决大多数常见的客户问题,提升客服人员响应速度,帮助卖家解决与客户之间的时差问题。此外,智能客服还支持一对多、全球主流语言的对话服务,随时切换多重身份,化身为智能客服、企业网站向导、购物助手、折扣优惠提取、答疑解惑、用户信息管理员等不同角色。因此,智能客服产品的应用可以节省大量的人力成本。

The intelligent customer service is especially suitable for high-tech product sellers because such products have high thresholds, relatively small competition and high profit margin. And consumers will encounter many problems in the process of using them. The intelligent customer service can integrate common problems of products, accurately respond to buyers and effectively improve customer service timeliness and quality.

智能客服平台尤其适合高科技产品卖家,因为此类产品门槛高,竞争相对较小,利润空间高,但是消费者在使用高科技产品的过程中会遇到很多问题。智能客服平台可以整合常见的产品问题,精确回复买家,有效提升客服的时效和质量。

The intelligent customer service is also very suitable for multi-platform sellers. It can centralize the customers of Amazon, eBay, Wish to a unified management platform, which can help sellers and buyers to establish strong links and improve efficiency. Moreover, the intelligent customer service is independent of the e-commerce platform and is not restricted to any e-commerce platform. For example,

Amazon in-station messages often delete the seller's phone number and external links in case of sales outflows. On the intelligent customer service, sellers' marketing can accurately target sticky buyers and potential buyers, eliminating the cost of advertisement.

智能客服平台也非常适合多平台卖家，可将亚马逊、易贝和 Wish 等平台的客户集中到一个平台统一管理，帮助卖家与买家建立起牢固的联系，提高运营效率。此外，智能客服平台独立于电商平台，不受任何电商平台的制约。比如亚马逊站内信经常删除卖家的电话和外部链接，以防销售外流。在智能客服平台上，卖家可以针对黏性买家和潜在买家进行精准营销，省去了广告费用。

Adapted from www.cifnews.com (改编自雨果网)

# Appendix
## Other Cross-Border E-Commerce Platforms

其他跨境电商
平台汇总

# Asia
# 亚 洲

## DHgate（敦煌网）

Founded in 2004 by Shutong Wang, DHgate was originally designed to connect Chinese SMEs with foreign SMEs and establish an online Silk Road to make online transactions easier, safer and more efficient. DHgate is the first website in China to provide B2B online transactions for SMEs. The main categories include electronic products, clothing, watches and jewelry, shoes and hats, and household items, etc. At present, DHgate has more than 1.7 million registered suppliers, with more than 7.7 million online products and over 15 million registered buyers, covering more than 220 countries and regions around the world. Both individual sellers and corporate sellers can register to sell.

敦煌网由王树彤创立于2004年,初衷是将中国中小企业与国外中小企业对接,建立网上丝绸之路,让在线交易变得更加简单、安全、高效。敦煌网是国内首个为中小企业提供B2B网上交易的网站,主营类目包括电子产品、服饰、钟表首饰、鞋帽箱包、家居用品等。目前敦煌网拥有170多万家累计注册供应商,在线产品数量超过770万,累计注册买家超过1500万,覆盖全球220余个国家和地区。个人卖家和企业卖家均可入驻。

## JollyChic（执御）

Founded in 2013, JollyChic is headquartered in Hangzhou, Zhejiang Province. It is currently the most well-known mobile e-commerce company in the Middle East. It is mainly engaged in clothing, shoes, accessories, home, mother & child items, body care and 3C Products. The registered users have exceeded 30 million, with nearly 5 billion of sales volume. The main consumer groups are very young and usually between 18 and 34 years old. JollyChic adopts the cross-border B2B2C mode, and the supplier enters the platform in the form of supplying products. The supplier only needs to be responsible for product uploading and timely delivery to the warehouse of the platform according to the order. Only enterprises with no less than 500,000 yuan registered capital and over one year's establishment time are eligible to enter.

执御成立于2013年，总部位于浙江杭州，是目前中东地区知名度最高、综合排名第一的移动端电商，主营服装、鞋包、配饰、家居、母婴童玩、美体护肤与3C类产品，注册用户已超3000万，销售额近50亿元。主要消费人群的年龄层集中在18—34岁，非常年轻。执御采用跨境B2B2C模式，供应商以供货方形式入驻平台，只需负责商品上传和根据订单及时发货至平台集货仓即可。仅限注册资金不低于50万元，并且成立满1年的企业入驻。

## Club Factory

Launched in 2016, Club Factory is headquartered in Hangzhou, Zhejiang Province, covering 29 countries including India, Southeast Asia and the Middle East. It is a cross-border e-commerce independent export platform. With more than 80 million users, Club Factory is currently the top three e-commerce platform in India, specializing in apparel, shoes, jewelry, home decoration, handbags, beauty products, gadgets and appliances. Entering Club Factory is relatively simple and sellers are required to have a business license.

Club Factory上线于2016年，总部位于浙江杭州，覆盖印度、东南亚地区、中东地区等29个国家，是一款跨境电商独立站出口平台。Club Factory拥有8000多万用户，目前是印度排名前三的电商平台，主营服装、鞋子、珠宝、家居装饰、手袋、美容产品、小工具和电器等产品。入驻Club Factory相对简单，卖家需要具备企业营业执照。

## Lazada（来赞达）

Founded in Singapore in 2012, Lazada is one of the largest online shopping sites in Southeast Asia. The best-selling categories include women's wear, accessories, beauty, mother & child items, shoes, bags, 3C accessories and home essentials. At present, Lazada has an average daily user visit of 4.5 million, with more than 20,000 merchants, and the level of competition among merchants is still relatively low. Lazada has six stations including Malaysia, Singapore, Indonesia, the Philippines, Thailand and Vietnam. In addition to Vietnam, the other five sites are open to Chinese e-commerce. New sellers need to register in Malaysia station first. According to the performance, Lazada will consider inviting sellers to open other sites.

来赞达于2012年成立于新加坡，是东南亚地区最大的在线购物网站之一，热卖品类包括女装、配饰、美妆、母婴、鞋品、箱包、3C配件和家居类等。来赞达平台日均用户访问量达到450万，拥有超过2万商家，入驻商家之间的竞争程度仍相对较低。来赞达有马来西亚、新加坡、印度尼西亚、菲律宾、泰国以及越南共6个站点，除了越南站，其他5个站点都对中国电商开放。新卖家需要先入驻马来西亚站，根据业绩情况，来赞达会考虑邀请卖家开通其他站点。

# Shopee（虾皮购物）

Founded in Singapore in 2015, Shopee is an e-commerce platform for Southeast Asia and Taiwan. It then expanded to markets in Malaysia, Thailand, Indonesia, Vietnam and the Philippines, etc. Shopee specializes in electronics, home, beauty care, mother & child items, apparel and fitness equipment. Shopee community has more than 30 million fans, 7 million active sellers and over 8,000 employees. It is the fastest growing e-commerce platform in Southeast Asia and the preferred platform for domestic exports to Southeast Asia. Taiwan and Malaysia are the preferred stations on shopee, and Shopee is currently the most mature platform with more orders.

虾皮购物于2015年在新加坡创立，是东南亚与中国台湾等市场电商平台，随后拓展至马来西亚、泰国、印度尼西亚、越南及菲律宾等地。虾皮购物主营电子产品、家居、美容保健、母婴、服饰及健身器材等品类。虾皮购物社群媒体粉丝数量超过3000万，拥有700万活跃卖家，员工超8000人，是东南亚发展最快的新兴电商平台，也是国货出海东南亚的首选平台。中国台湾和马来西亚是入驻虾皮购物的首选站点，也是虾皮购物目前最成熟、单量多及出单最容易的两个站点。

# Qoo10（趣天网）

Qoo10 is Singapore's largest e-commerce platform and the second most popular mobile shopping App with 7.1 million visitors. It is famous for its cheap goods. The platform has a wide range of products, including electronic accessories, clothing, food, tickets, etc. It is considered as the Singapore version of Taobao. The company has operated seven shopping platforms in five countries including Japan and Singapore, and it continues to develop in other Asian countries and regions. To settle in Qoo10, sllers need to have business licenses, UnionPay cards that accept Singapore dollar, and proof to show experience in other cross-border e-commerce platforms.

趣天网是新加坡第一大电商平台、第二大常用的移动购物App，拥有710万访客，以廉价商品出名，平台商品种类繁多，包括了电子配件、服装、食品、门票等，被视为新加坡版的淘宝。该公司已在日本和新加坡等5个国家运营了7个购物平台，还在继续向其他亚洲国家和地区发展。入驻趣天网需具备企业营业执照、接受新元的银联卡和其他跨境电商平台的运营经验。

## Zalora

Founded in 2012 and headquartered in Singapore, Zalora is an online fashion and beauty product shopping platform that provides fashion, accessories, footwear and skin care products for men and women. There are currently more than 500 brands on Zalora, with sites in 11 countries and regions including Singapore, Australia, New Zealand, Indonesia, Malaysia, Thailand, Vietnam, etc. Zalora is one of the fastest growing fashion e-commerce companies in Southeast Asia, with approximately 5 million monthly website visits. Zalora Marketplace allows suppliers and small and medium-sized businesses to create online store with their own brands on the platform. The customer manager of the platform will support the seller's operations and maintenance. Sellers who want to join the platform can contact the business manager or apply to become a seller directly on the official website.

Zalora成立于2012年，总部位于新加坡，是一个在线时装及美容产品购物平台，为男女顾客提供时装、饰物、鞋履及化妆护肤品。目前入驻品牌有500余个，在新加坡、澳大利亚、新西兰、印度尼西亚、马来西亚、泰国、越南等11个国家和地区设置站点。Zalora是东南亚成长速度最快的时尚类电商之一，目前每月网站访问人数约500万。Zalora Marketplace允许供应商和中小商家在平台内创建自己的品牌店面，平台的客户经理会对卖家的运营和维护工作予以支持。想要入驻的卖家可以与招商经理联系，也可以直接在官网申请成为卖家。

## Gmarket

Gmarket is Korea's largest e-commerce platform and a subsidiary of eBay. The hot-selling categories include apparel, electronics, food and beverage, home, makeup, and leisure sports. The company currently operates in nearly 100 countries around the world. Gmarket has more than 20 million members and 8.45 million independent visits. More than 64% of Korean consumers are shopping on Gmarket. The customers are mainly 20 to 30 years old. At present, Chinese sellers can enter Gmarket directly and quickly through ESG.

Gmarket是韩国最大的电商平台，是易贝旗下的子公司，热销品类包括服装、电子产品、食物饮料、家居、化妆美容、休闲运动等,目前业务覆盖全球近100个国家和地区。Gmarket拥有2000多万会员及845万月独立访客量,超过64%的韩国消费者在Gmarket进行线上购物,客户以20—30岁的人群为主。目前,中国卖家可以通过ESG,直接快速地入驻Gmarket开店。

## 11Street（11番街区）

11Street is a well-known e-commerce platform, subsidiary of South Korea's mobile communication giant SK. It is the second largest comprehensive shopping website in Korean retail market, next only to Gmarket, with a transaction volume of $8.4 billion in 2017. There are many high-quality goods on 11Street. The website users cover more than one-third of Koreans, mainly from 20 to 40 years old. The number of mobile users is also among the top three in the Korean e-commerce platform. In 2018, the trading volume of Single's Day was 120 million US dollars, which set a new record for the trading volume of Korean e-commerce platform. Sellers with corporate qualifications can apply for entry, and the company needs to have a corporate business account that can collect dollars.

11番街区是韩国移动通信巨头SK旗下的知名电商平台,是韩国零售市场中排名第二的综合性购物网站,仅次于Gmarket,2017年交易额为84亿美元。11番街区里面拥有许多优质商品,网站用户覆盖了超过三分之一的韩国人,主要为20—40岁的人群,移动用户数也在韩国电商平台中位列前三。2018年"双十一"活动当日交易额为1.2亿美元,刷新了韩国电商平台交易额的历史新高。具备企业资质的卖家可申请入驻,企业需要拥有对公美元收款账户。

## Rakuten（日本乐天）

Founded in 1997, Rakuten is the largest e-commerce company in Japan and a world-renowned e-commerce giant. At present, Chinese sellers have the priority to operate online store in US, French and German stations on Rakuten. The entry requirements and procedures are different according to stations. Unlike Amazon, which is product centered, Rakuten is store centered. Rakuten's philosophy is to serve the sellers well and let the sellers fully exert their subjective initiative to establish real connections with the buyers.

日本乐天成立于1997年,是日本最大的电商公司,也是世界知名的电商巨头。目前中国卖家可以优先入驻的日本乐天有美国、法国和德国站,不同站点有不同的入驻要求和流程。不同于亚马逊以产品为中心,日本乐天则以店铺为中心,其理念是服务好卖家,让卖家充分发挥主观能动性去和买家建立真实的联系。

## Flipkart

Flipkart was founded in 2007 by two former Amazon employees, Sachin Bansal and Binny Bansal, and it is India's largest e-commerce platform. At first, the platform focused on book sales, and then expanded to other products such as electronics, apparel, and fashion, etc. As of 2017, Flipkart's market share in India had reached 39.5%, the number of users exceeded 1 billion, and the number of visitors per month is 69.8 million. It will be relatively complicated for Chinese sellers to join Flipkart and it requires additional information such as the Indian Tax Registration Number (GSTIN).

Flipkart是由亚马逊的两名前员工萨钦·班萨尔和比尼·班萨尔于2007年创建的,是印度最大的电子商务平台。起初平台专注于图书销售,之后扩展到电子产品、服饰、时尚等其他产品。截至2017年,Flipkart在印度本土的市场占有率达39.5%,用户数量超过10亿,月访客数高达6980万。中国卖家入驻Flipkart会比较复杂,需要有印度税务登记号(GSTIN)等其他信息。

## Paytm Mall

Founded in August 2010 by Vijay Shekhar Sharma, Paytm is India's largest mobile payment and business platform with a core business of offering online payment services. In February 2017, Paytm launched Paytm Mall, officially entering the e-commerce field, selling products including electronic accessories, mobile phones, fashion apparel, household items, accessories, jewelry, electrical appliances, mother & baby items, etc. More than 75,000 merchants have joined the platform, and the monthly sales have exceeded $250 million. Paytm Mall has opened a special channel for Chinese sellers. Individual sellers can find an agent in India to assist in the opening of the store. The business sellers can contact business manager of the platform or directly register online.

Paytm是由维杰·谢哈尔·夏尔马于2010年8月创立的,是印度最大的移动支付和商务平台,核心业务是提供在线支付服务。2017年2月,Paytm推出Paytm Mall,正式进入电子商务领域,销售的产品包括电子配件、手机、时尚服饰、家居用品、配件、珠宝、电器、母婴等。平台已经有超过75000家商家入驻,月销售额也超过了2.5亿美元。Paytm Mall对中国卖家开通了专门的渠道,个人卖家可以找印度的代理企业协助开店,企业卖家可以联系平台的招商经理或者自主线上注册开通。

## Souq

Founded in 2005, Souq is headquartered in Dubai and is known as the Middle East version of Amazon in the Middle East. It currently has four stations in Dubai, Saudi, Egypt and Kuwait. With 6 million users and 10 million independent visits per month, Souq specializes in 31 categories including electronics, fashion, health, mother & child items and household items, etc. In 2015, the sales of Souq reach approximately $75 billion and the total financing was $390 million. Chinese sellers need to go through third-party channels to join Souq.

Souq成立于2005年,总部位于迪拜,被称为是中东版的亚马逊,目前共设有迪拜站、沙特站、埃及站以及科威特站四个站点。Souq拥有600万用户和每月1000万独立访问量,主营电子产品、时尚美容、养生、母婴和家居用品等31个类目。2015年,Souq销售额约750亿美元,总融资额为3.9亿美元。中国卖家入驻Souq需要通过第三方渠道。

## Daraz

Founded in 2012, Daraz is Pakistan's most popular online shopping platform, covering Bangladesh, Myanmar, Sri Lanka and Nepal. Daraz started out as a fashion e-commerce company and currently specializes in electronics, clothing, cosmetics, auto replacement parts, and various daily necessities. At present, the Daraz Pakistan site is open to high quality sellers of the Jumia & Linio platform. The platform does not require any participation fees, security deposits and annual fees, and no commission is charged for the moment.

Daraz成立于2012年,是巴基斯坦国内最受欢迎的网上购物平台,该平台业务还覆盖孟加拉国、缅甸、斯里兰卡和尼泊尔等国。Daraz是由时尚电商起家,目前主营电子产品、服装、化妆品、汽车配件、各种生活用品等各大品类。目前Daraz巴基斯坦站点向Jumia & Linio平台的优质卖家开放,平台前期无须任何入驻费、保证金和年费,暂不收取佣金。

# North America
# 北美洲

## Wayfair Inc.

Wayfair Inc. is the largest home e-commerce company in the United States with annual sales exceeding $3 billion. Its predecessor was the CNS Stores, which was established in 2002. Now it sells furniture, household goods, lamps, decorations and other products, with more than 80,000 products from more than 10,000 suppliers. Wayfair's main customers are aged between 35 and 65 years old, with the family income of $50,000 to $250,000. Headquartered in Boston, Massachusetts, Wayfair has offices and warehouses in the United States, Canada, Germany, Ireland and Britain. Wayfair has different brands: Wayfair.com, which sells mid-range furniture; AllModern, which sells high-end brands; Joss & Main, is a designer flash sale site, as well as DwellStudio and Birch Lane, etc. They all have different customer groups. Sellers with corporate qualifications can apply to join and products are delivered from overseas warehouses.

Wayfair Inc.是美国最大的家居电商,年销售额超30亿,其前身是2002年成立的CNS Stores。现在它销售家具、居家用品、灯具、装饰品等产品,拥有1万余家供应商的超过8万种产品。Wayfair的主要客户群体是35—65岁、家庭年收入5万—25万美元的女性。Wayfair总部位于马萨诸塞州的波士顿,在美国、加拿大、德国、爱尔兰和英国设有办事处和仓库。Wayfair旗下有不同定位的品牌:Wayfair.com以销售中档家具为主,AllModern以销售高端品牌为主,Joss & Main是一个设计师款的闪购网站,还有DwellStudio和Birch Lane等,它们均面向不同的客群。具备企业资质的卖家可以申请入驻,货物从海外仓派送。

## Overstock

Founded in 1999, Overstock is a well-known online shopping platform and brand discount platform in the United States, mainly selling household items, jewelry, electronic products, clothing, books and audiovisual products, etc. At present, Overstock products have been sold to 180 countries and regions around the world.

The users on Overstock are mainly people with middle or high income, with 76% of women, and 35 million visitors per month. The price per order is relatively high. Overstock buyers are mainly located in the United States, accounting for more than 85%, followed by Japan, Canada, Britain, France and India. Overstock platform requires sellers to have a registered company in the US, and has a certain sales record on Amazon, eBay and other large platforms.

Overstock 创立于1999年,是美国当地非常知名的网上购物平台和品牌折扣销售平台,主要销售家居用品、珠宝、电子产品、服装、图书和音像制品等。目前,Overstock的产品已经销往了全球180个国家和地区。Overstock上的用户以中高收入者为主,女性占76%,每个月的访客可达到3500万,客单价也比较高。Overstock买家主要分布在美国,占比达到85%以上,随后是日本、加拿大、英国、法国和印度。Overstock平台要求卖家在美国有注册公司,并且在亚马逊和易贝等大平台上有一定的销售记录。

## 沃尔玛（Walmart）

Walmart is headquartered in Arkansas, USA. It is mainly involved in the retail industry, with strong off-line resources and e-commerce logistics advantages. Walmart Drop Ship Vendor can help sellers quickly clear inventory, which is equivalent to Amazon VE or VC. Walmart has a Warehouse Supplier and DSV. Walmart suspended attracting investment in China in October of 2017. In March 2018, it began to rectify the suspected Chinese sellers on the platform. At present, the entry of Walmart DSV is open to US companies.

沃尔玛总部位于美国阿肯色州,主要涉足零售业,拥有强大的线下渠道资源及电商物流优势。沃尔玛DSV可以帮助卖家快速清理库存,相当于亚马逊VE或VC。沃尔玛有自营发货和供应商发货。沃尔玛在2017年10月暂停了在中国的招商,2018年3月份又开始了对平台上违规的疑似中国卖家展开了整顿,目前沃尔玛DSV的入驻对美国公司是开放的。

## Tophatter

Tophatter is an online auction e-commerce platform in the United States that sells products such as electronics, jewelry, clothing, household goods, and toys. The platform mainly has two sales modes, including auction and buy it now, which is the fastest selling platform. Most of the orders are sold through 90-second real-time auction. At present, Tophatter has mobile app and website, and the mobile app accounts for more than 95% of the traffic. Opening a store in Tophatter is simple and currently it only allows companies to join.

Tophatter 是美国的一个在线拍卖电商平台,主要销售电子产品、珠宝饰品、服装、家居、玩具等品类的商品。平台主要有两种销售模式,包括拍卖和一口价,是销售速度最快的平台,订单大部分都是通过90秒实时拍卖的方式卖出。目前 Tophatter 有手机端,也有 Web 端,手机端占了95%以上的流量。在 Tophatter 开店很简单,目前仅支持公司入驻。

## Newegg (新蛋网)

Founded in 2001, Newegg is headquartered in Los Angeles, USA, and sells computer and peripherals, consumer electronics, mobile phones, home appliances, office equipment, digital products, gaming, multimedia and other technology products. With more than 30 million loyal users in the US, it is one of the largest IT digital retailers. Newegg in the US does not restrict the entry of brands, and only companies are allowed to join. It requires link that has sales record and feedback of eBay or Amazon as a reference.

新蛋网创立于2001年,总部位于美国洛杉矶,主要销售电脑及周边配件、消费类电子产品、手机、家电、办公设备、数码产品、游戏设备、多媒体等科技产品及其他日用产品。在美国拥有3000多万忠诚度极高的用户,是全美规模上最大的 IT 数码类零售商之一。新蛋网开店不限制入驻品牌,仅限企业入驻,要求提供易贝或亚马逊平台链接的销售记录及评价作为参考。

## Tanga

Tanga is an American comprehensive e-commerce platform. The most popular categories include pets, household goods, hairdressing, beauty, electronics, etc. The main products are discounted products, and users' stickiness is high. The best sales volume products on Tanga are between $10 and $30, and the platform does not have account restrictions. It can quickly help sellers decrease inventory and re-sell through multiple social platforms. Sellers list products at wholesale prices, and Tanga will intelligently price each item to match customers with personalized and advanced customer segmentation capabilities. The platform is limited to enterprises, and it requires certain operating experience on platforms such as Amazon or eBay.

Tanga 是一个美国全品类电商平台,最受欢迎的品类包括宠物、家居、美发、美妆、电子产品等,主攻打折产品,用户黏性强。Tanga 上均价在10—30美元之间的产品销量最优,平台不进行账号限制,可以快速帮助卖家消耗库存,同时通过多渠道社交平台对用户进行再销售。卖家以批发价列出商品,Tanga 会智能定价,通过个性化和先进的客户细分功能将每个列表与顾客进行匹配。平台仅限企业入驻,需要有一定亚马逊或易贝等平台的运营经验。

## OpenSky

OpenSky is an emerging niche e-commerce platform in the United States, with a focus on high-income women aged 35 to 65. According to Similarweb, OpenSky has about 1 million pageviews per month. OpenSky currently has 10 million active users and 100,000 sellers, with annual sales exceeding $5 billion. In 2015, Alibaba made a strategic investment in OpenSky and currently owns 37% of OpenSky. In 2017, OpenSky began to attract investment from China. The company must have a US Federal Tax Number (EIN), an international credit card, and a US address for product return.

OpenSky 是美国新兴的一个小众电商平台,主要客户群体集中在 35—65 岁的高收入女性。根据 Similarweb 的统计,OpenSky 每个月浏览量约 100 万。目前 OpenSky 有 1000 万活跃用户和 10 万卖家,每年销售额超过 50 亿美元。2015 年阿里巴巴对 OpenSky 进行战略投资,目前拥有 OpenSky 37% 的股权。2017 年 OpenSky 开始对华招商,入驻企业需要有美国联邦税号(EIN)、国际信用卡和美国退货地址。

# Europe
# 欧洲

## Yandex

Yandex is one of Russia's important network service portals and is currently the largest e-commerce platform in Russia. It is like Alibaba in Russia. Yandex is mainly engaged in electronic products, household items, household appliances, clothing and bags. To enter Yandex, sellers need to have business license, and preferably know Russian. Sellers also need to register Yandex account and the commission rate is 1%.

Yandex 是俄罗斯重要网络服务门户之一,目前也是俄罗斯本土最大的电商平台,相当于俄罗斯的阿里巴巴。Yandex 主营电子产品、家居用品、家用电器、服饰箱包等产品。卖家入驻 Yandex 需要有企业营业执照,最好懂俄语,并且要提前注册 Yandex 账号,其佣金低至 1%。

## Umka

Launched in 2016, Umka is one of the largest online shopping sites for Chinese goods in Russian speaking countries, covering 12 countries with approximately 350 million consumers. At present, the categories that Chinese sellers can sell household goods, home appliances, hardware and building materials, 3C, auto parts and outdoor products, etc. Sellers can apply directly on the official website. The background for Umka's seller is Chinese and the product information can be translated by the platform professional team.

Umka 于 2016 年推出,是俄语地区最大的中国商品在线购物网站之一,覆盖俄语区 12 个国家,拥有约 3.5 亿的消费者。目前中国卖家可以入驻的类目有家居、家电、五金建材、3C、汽配和户外产品等,卖家可以直接在官网申请入驻。Umka 的卖家后台为中文,产品信息可以由平台专业团队进行翻译。

## Joom

Launched in 2016, Joom is currently focusing on Russian and other European countries and is expanding the South African market. It is a fast-growing mobile shopping platform. Joom is characterized by small competition, high volume, low price per order and rapid development. At present, there are fewer Chinese sellers. Sellers who want to sell on Joom need to have corporate qualifications and certain cross-border e-commerce experience. Seller enters the waiting list after completing the application form, and then waits for further notice from the platform.

Joom 于 2016 年上线,目前主要针对俄罗斯与其他欧洲国家,正在拓展南非市场,是一个快速增长的移动端购物平台。Joom 的特点是竞争小、单量高、客单价低、发展快,目前中国卖家比较少。入驻 Joom 的卖家需要有企业资质和一定跨境电商运营经验,卖家在填写申请表后先进入等候名单,再等待平台进一步的通知。

## Cdiscount

Founded in 1999, Cdiscount is the largest e-commerce platform in France. It is mainly wholesale and has price advantage. The current business includes daily necessities, food, electronic products, household appliances, mother and child items, luggage, toys, etc. Cdiscount also has stations in Colombia, Ivory Coast, Ecuador, Thailand, Vietnam, Senegal, Brazil, Cameroon and Panama. The requirement to sell on Cdiscount is high. Sellers need to have enterprise qualification and email customer service personnel who can speak French. The seller's application from any country may be rejected, and the specific application standard is also confidential.

Cdiscount成立于1999年,是法国最大的电子商务平台,以批发为主,价格比较有优势。目前经营范围包括日用品、食品、电子产品、家用电器、母婴用品、箱包、玩具等。Cdiscount在哥伦比亚、科特迪瓦、厄瓜多尔、泰国、越南、塞内加尔、巴西、喀麦隆、巴拿马等国也有分站。入驻Cdiscount的要求较高,需要卖家具备企业资质且必须有会法语的电子邮件客服人员,任何国家的卖家入驻申请都有可能被拒绝,并且具体的申请标准也是保密的。

## PriceMinister

Founded in 2000, PriceMinister is headquartered in France and is the second most visited e-commerce site in France. It specializes in 3C, fashion and home categories. Joining in PriceMinister requires a business license, certificate of brand or certificate of attorney, as well as operators who can speak French and have certain e-commerce experience. Chinese sellers need to be verified by ESG before they enter.

PriceMinister成立于2000年,总部位于法国,是法国访问量排名第二的电子商务网站,主营3C、时尚及家居等品类。入驻PriceMinister需要拥有企业营业执照、品牌证书或授权书、会法语的运营人员和一定的电商经营经验。中国卖家需要通过ESG集团的审核才能入驻。

## Fnac

Fnac is the third largest e-commerce platform in France. It specializes in cultural products and electrical products and has more than 6 million online members. Chinese sellers can join Fnac through the ESG Group.

Fnac是法国第三大电商平台,主营文化产品和电器产品,拥有600多万的线上会员。中国卖家可以通过ESG集团入驻Fnac。

## La Redoute (乐都特)

La Redoute is the best e-commerce site for French clothing and home decoration, with more than 7 million independent visitors per month. La Redoute is also active internationally, covering more than 120 countries and has 13 million active customers. The platform has certain requirements for the seller's French skill and the transactions are paid in Euro.

乐都特是法国服装和家居装饰的最佳电商网站，每月有超过700万的独立访客。乐都特在国际上也很活跃，覆盖120多个国家，拥有1300万活跃顾客。平台对卖家的法语有一定要求，交易以欧元结算。

## Allegro

Founded in 1999, Allegro is the largest e-commerce platform in Poland, initially an auction site. Allegro has 14 million users, 90% of whom regularly shop at Allegro, with an average of 300,000 active users per day. Depending on whether the seller chooses a personal account or a corporate account, different document is required for registration and different accounts enjoy different rights.

Allegro成立于1999年，是波兰最大的电商平台，最初是拍卖型网站。Allegro拥有1400万用户，90%的用户定期在Allegro购物，日均活跃用户30万。根据选择的是个人账户还是企业账户，卖家注册的时候需要提供不同资料，享有不同权利。

## Bol.com

Founded in 1999, Bol.com is the largest e-commerce platform in Netherlands, Belgium and Luxembourg. It has 7.5 million active customers and more than 1 million daily visits. Bol. com specializes in books, toys and electronics, and the operation is like Amazon. Sellers need to register to have their buyers' accounts on the official website if they want to join Bol.com.

Bol.com成立于1999年，是荷兰、比利时、卢森堡地区最大的电商平台，拥有750万活跃客户，日访问量超过100万次。Bol.com主营书籍、玩具和电子产品等，运营方式类似亚马逊。想要入驻Bol.com的卖家需要先在官网注册买家账户。

## Fruugo

Launched in Finland in 2010, Fruugo is an international e-commerce platform that sells products to 32 European and American countries and the transactions are settled in local currency. Fruugo has 1 million loyal users and 7.5 million pageviews per month. The user stickiness and buyer's consumption level are relatively high. Fruugo specializes in electronics, sports, fashion, beauty & health, and gardening.

Sellers need to register for UK VAT and have an international product list if they want to join Fruugo.

Fruugo 于 2010 年在芬兰推出，是一个国际电商平台，主要面向 32 个欧美国家销售，并以本国货币结算。Fruugo 拥有 100 万忠实用户，每月有 750 万浏览量，用户黏性高，买家的消费层次相对较高，主营电子产品、运动、时尚、美容健康、生活园艺等产品。入驻 Fruugo 前卖家需要先注册英国 VAT 和拥有国际化的产品清单。

## Zalando

Founded in Berlin, Germany in 2008, Zalando specializes in fashion, shoes and accessories. Zalando has 14.7 million active customers and has over 100 million monthly visits. The business covers 15 European countries including Germany, Austria, France, Italy, Spain and Britain. Sellers who want to join need to have business license and their own brand or brand authorization. Sellers can contact the official business manager directly or find an agent to join Zalando.

Zalando 于 2008 年在德国柏林成立，主营时装、鞋、配件等产品。Zalando 拥有 1470 万活跃客户，月访问量超 1 亿次。业务覆盖德国、奥地利、法国、意大利、西班牙、英国等 15 个欧洲国家。想要入驻的卖家需要有营业执照和自有品牌或品牌授权，可以直接联系官方招商经理或找代理公司。

# Africa
# 非洲

## Jumia

Founded in 2012, Jumia is an African e-commerce giant, covering 11 countries including Nigeria, Morocco, Egypt, Kenya, Pakistan and Colo d'Ivoire, etc. Jumia's main categories include fashion products, electronic products, mother and kid items, books and so on. A business license and a Payoneer business account are required to join Jumia.

Jumia 成立于 2012 年，是非洲电子商务巨头，主要覆盖尼日利亚、摩洛哥、埃及、肯尼亚、科特迪瓦等 11 个国家。Jumia 主营品类包括时尚产品、电子产品、母婴用品、书籍等。入驻 Jumia 时卖家需要有营业执照和 Payoneer 企业账号。

## Kilimall

Founded in 2014, Kilimall is a large e-commerce platform founded by former Huawei employee in Kenya. It also opened sites in Nigeria and Uganda, covering 280 million people. The customer base is small wholesale sellers and retail buyers, aged between 20 and 30. Both corporate sellers and individual sellers can join Kilimall.

Kilimall创立于2014年,是由原华为员工在肯尼亚创办的一家大型电商平台,在尼日利亚和乌干达也开设了站点,覆盖2.8亿人口。客户群体是小型批发卖家和零售买家,年龄范围在20—30岁。企业卖家和个人卖家都可以入驻Kilimall平台。

## Konga

Founded in Nigeria in 2012, Konga is a Nigerian e-commerce giant that specializes in mother and child items, healthcare and personal care. Currently, it only has sites in Nigeria. In 2014, Konga opened a third-party seller channel. Now, there are 1 million website users and 300,000 daily visits.

Konga于2012年成立于尼日利亚,是尼日利亚电商巨头,主营母婴用品、医疗保健、个人护理等产品,目前只在尼日利亚开设了站点。2014年Konga开通了第三方卖家入驻渠道,目前网站用户100万,日访问量30万。

# South America
# 南美洲

## Linio

Founded in 2012 and headquartered in Mexico, Linio is the largest B2C e-commerce platform in Latin America and currently has offices in Shenzhen. Linio has opened seven sites in Argentina, Chile, Colombia, Ecuador, Mexico, Panama and Peru, etc., having more than 6 million social fans. The main categories include electronics, household goods, fashion, beauty and health products and baby products. Linio only charges a commission, instead of monthly fee or membership fee.

Linio成立于2012年,总部位于墨西哥,是拉丁美洲最大的B2C电商平台,目前在深圳设有办公室。Linio 开通了阿根廷、智利、哥伦比亚、厄瓜多尔、墨西哥、巴拿马和秘鲁 7 个站点,平台拥有 600 多万的社交粉丝。主营类目包括电子产品、家居用品、时装、美容健康产品和婴幼儿产品。Linio 不收取卖家月租费或会员费,只收取佣金。

## MercadoLibre

Founded in Uruguay in 1999, MercadoLibre is the largest e-commerce ecosystem in Latin America. It currently covers 19 Latin American countries including Brazil, Argentina, Mexico, Chile and Colombia, etc. It is the seventh most visited retail website in the world. The hot items on the platform include electronics & accessories, mobile phones, fashion, home & garden, auto parts and sports equipment. The seller who wants to join the platform must contact the business manager to activate the account after creating an account on the official website.

MercadoLibre 于 1999 年在乌拉圭创立,是拉丁美洲最大的电子商务生态系统,目前业务范围已覆盖巴西、阿根廷、墨西哥、智利、哥伦比亚等 19 个拉丁美洲国家,是世界上访问量排名第七的零售网站。平台热销品类包括电子及配件、手机、时尚、家居与园艺、汽车配件和运动用品等。申请入驻的卖家需在官网创建账户后联系招商经理进行激活。

## Oceania
## 大洋洲

## Trade Me

Founded in 1999, Trade Me is New Zealand's largest e-commerce platform. Trade Me is similar to Taobao in China. There are a large number of third-party sellers. It mainly sells clothing, electronic accessories, furniture and daily necessities. Trade Me has 3/4 of New Zealand traffic and the customers are very sticky. Joining Trade Me is free. The current commission is 7.9% of the seller's monthly income and logistics costs, with an upper limit of $149 per month.

Trade Me 成立于 1999 年,是新西兰最大的电商平台。Trade Me 类似于中国的淘宝,有大量第三方卖家,主营服饰、电子配件、家具生活用品等。Trade Me 拥有新西兰 3/4 的流量,用户黏性也很高。入驻 Trade me 是免费的,目前所收的佣金是卖家当月收入加上物流费用的 7.9%,上限是 149 美元/月。

# References

［1］王琼. 跨境电商实用英语［M］. 北京:中国人民大学出版社,2018.

［2］易传识网络科技. 跨境电商多平台运营［M］. 北京:电子工业出版社,2015.

［3］易露霞,尤彧聪. 跨境电子商务双语教程［M］. 北京:清华大学出版社,2019.

［4］徐凡. 跨境电子商务基础与实务(中英双语版)［M］. 北京:中国铁道出版社,2019.

［5］李鹏博. 揭秘跨境电商［M］. 北京:电子工业出版社,2015.

［6］速卖通大学. 跨境电商SNS营销与商机［M］. 北京:电子工业出版社,2018.

［7］马述忠,卢传胜,丁红朝,等. 跨境电商理论与实务［M］. 杭州:浙江大学出版社,2018.

图书在版编目(CIP)数据

　跨境电商入门一本通:汉英对照 / 陈一宁编著. —杭州:浙
江工商大学出版社,2020.11
　ISBN 978-7-5178-3833-3

　Ⅰ. ①跨… Ⅱ. ①陈 Ⅲ. ①电子商务—商业经营—汉、英
Ⅳ. ①F713.365.2

　中国版本图书馆 CIP 数据核字(2020)第073045号

**跨境电商入门一本通(汉英对照)**
KUAJING DIANSHANG RUMEN YI BEN TONG (HANYING DUIZHAO)
陈一宁 编著

| | | |
|---|---|---|
| **责任编辑** | 张莉娅　姚　媛 | |
| **封面设计** | 叶泽雯 | |
| **责任印制** | 包建辉 | |
| **出版发行** | 浙江工商大学出版社 | |
| | （杭州市教工路198号　邮政编码310012） | |
| | （E-mail: zjgsupress@163.com） | |
| | （网址:http://www.zjgsupress.com） | |
| | 电话:0571-88904980,88831806(传真) | |
| **排　版** | 杭州朝曦图文设计有限公司 | |
| **印　刷** | 杭州高腾印务有限公司 | |
| **开　本** | 787mm×1092mm　1/16 | |
| **印　张** | 12.25 | |
| **字　数** | 246千 | |
| **版 印 次** | 2020年11月第1版　2020年11月第1次印刷 | |
| **书　号** | ISBN 978-7-5178-3833-3 | |
| **定　价** | 50.00元 | |